The Damn Good Resume Guide

by Yana Parker

Ten Speed Press

The author wishes to acknowledge Hal Howard,
Carlene Cole, Rose Petty, Roger Pritchard,
Greg Gavin, Rich Hausman—and her resume clients
for their suggestions, which are incorporated
in this book.

1

TEN SPEED PRESS
P O Box 7123
Berkeley, California 94707

Library of Congress Catalog Card Number: 83-040079
ISBN: 0-89815-112-0

Cover design by Brenton Beck and Yana Parker
Illustrations by Ellen Sasaki
Beverly Anderson Graphic Design

Printed in the United States of America

9 10 — 90 89

Contents

LONG TIME INTEREST

For many years I've had a great interest in people's work lives and job satisfaction (including my own) and this first showed up in a three-year volunteer job as director/coordinator of a community Youth Employment Service. That led to a job with an upstate New York community college project to train "hard-core unemployed youth" (whatever *that* means) in job-related skills, and then on to a similar position as "Community Worker" with New York State employment offices in Albany, Troy and Schenectady, a job I really loved.

Later, living in California I noticed that many of the people in my personal network were involved in career counseling and small business development, and we'd do "brainstorming" and strategizing for the fun of it. Then in 1979 I decided to try self-employment using my writing skills and a new IBM Selectric typewriter, having resigned from office work in the big city to use my talents in a more personally rewarding way. I began by offering an editing, typing and business writing service out of my home in Oakland, but soon specialized in resumes, because it was "natural" for me, and because few people seemed to know how to do it well.

I never really set out to write or publish this book; it started out, in 1980, as just a few loose pages of instructions and examples, handed to clients as "homework" before we'd get together to work on their resume. (I'd grown weary of verbally giving the same instructions over and over, and finally wrote them down.)

THE HUMBLE "FREEBIE" GETS STATUS

In our "Briarpatch" self-help group of small business people there was a financial consultant, and one day I hired him to help me look critically at the fragile economics of my business. He noticed the packet of "homework" pages I gave to clients (now including sample resumes and a list of action verbs), and asked "Why are you *giving* this away? Don't you see that it's valuable, and that you could easily get a few dollars for it?"

So I took his advice, and at the same time expanded the packet and wrote up the instructions in greater detail. I designed a card-stock cover, stapled it together, and priced it at $2. Over the following year it got expanded twice more, and I began to suspect that it might be marketable as a how-to guide independently of my resume writing business. So I typed it up very carefully, added some graphics, designed a more professional cover, and persuaded two local bookstores to carry a few copies on consignment.

GETTING PUBLISHED

It turned out that Phil Wood, owner of Ten Speed Press, almost immediately found a copy in Cody's Bookstore in Berkeley, liked it, and proposed publishing it. Out of negotiations with him and George Young, it became clear that another section would be helpful: answers to the recurrent problems that come up when people attempt to write a resume. So I wrote that section, called "Ten Tough Questions," based on experience struggling with these dilemmas many times over. The section on employer acceptance, called "The Acid Test," was developed at the suggestion of Richard Bolles, author of *What Color Is Your Parachute?*, who pointed out the need to be sure that what was presented really served the reader in terms of employers' expectations. (Thank you, RB.)

It's three years later as I write this, and THE DAMN GOOD RESUME GUIDE has clearly become respected and popular in its field. Professional job counselors call it "the best available," a fair number of self-help job clubs and career development centers (and even college courses in psych and women's studies!) have made it "required reading," and people call from some amazing distances asking "Where can I get a copy?"

RESUMES AND WORD PROCESSING

Now I've come back again to offering a one-to-one resume service, after two years in another field. But this time I'm working on a wonderful computer, the Apple MACINTOSH. My clients and I write and edit directly on the screen, bypassing paper altogether, and it is wonderful to enjoy the flexibility and speed and professional appearance that comes with having a "word processing" tool. Also this time around, I've become convinced that the optional "Summary of Qualifications" or "Highlights of Qualifications" is so very effective that I'd *almost* call it a necessity.

All of the 12 new resumes in this edition were produced on the "Mac," and you can see that this word processing opens up some graphic options and offers space-conserving advantages. If you are willing to pay a little more to get your resume word-processed and stored on disc, then future revisions are relatively cheap and chan happen very easily and quickly—factors that often matter a lot. I highly recommend checking this out in your locality.

FOR CAREER COUNSELORS

Next on my agenda is a supplementary handbook for career counselors, showing them how to help their clients develop better resumes, faster and easier. (There's more about that, and the resume workshops I do, at the back of the book.)

Finally—I'd like to remind people that writing a resume *is* truly hard work, and remind them not to take it personally when they run up against how tough it is. Just "hang in there," knowing that you'll be MUCH more clear about what you're aiming for and about what you've got to offer after you go through this process. The end product, your resume, is a morale booster and a confidence builder, well worth all that sweat whether anybody else ever sees it or not.

Yana Parker
Berkeley, California
April 3, 1986

What is a Damn Good Resume?

A DAMN GOOD RESUME is a functional resume with a chronological job history. It starts with a clearly stated Job Objective, and then presents an assessment of your skills and experience in terms of that current objective. It is brief, focused, and effective.

In contrast, the old style "standard resume" listed, in chronological order, your job experiences, and the basic duties you performed under each job title. It usually omitted mention of your objective (incredible!). And worst of all, it was left to the potential employer to figure out what all that MEANT to her, what you wanted, how well suited you were for the position available.

A DAMN GOOD RESUME is designed to give you full credit for what you've learned and accomplished, regardless of where or when, regardless of job titles or pay.

And it's a refreshing RELIEF to the employer; she looks it over and sighs, "WOW, finally somebody who knows just what she wants, knows what she has to offer, and even seems to know what WE need too!"

4

A Damn Good Resume Has Four Basic Parts

* A clearly stated JOB OBJECTIVE

* A SKILL ASSESSMENT related directly to the Job Objective

* A listing of your WORK HISTORY

* A listing of your EDUCATION & TRAINING

A DAMN GOOD RESUME DOES NOT HAVE:

Personal information that's irrelevant to the job — age, marital status, height and weight, hobbies.
Vague references to a job objective — like "I want to work with people."
Jargon — like "interface."
A clutter of too-precise dates — we simply say "1971-1975."

HERE'S WHAT A DAMN GOOD RESUME CAN DO:

Focus attention on your strong points.
Minimize the impact of times when you were unemployed.
Demonstrate that you're a "pro" even if you've never been paid for what you do.
Show how you're well qualified for work in a different field from your present one.

The Basics

Getting Started

Start writing—with at least four sheets of paper, one for each of the four parts of your finished resume: Objective, Skills, Work History, Education & Training.

Type up your notes as you go along; a confusing mass of handwritten bits-and-pieces suddenly becomes manageable when it's neatly typed. Keep retyping as you edit; all at once, VOILA, it takes shape!

SAVE ALL YOUR NOTES! This is NOT the last resume you'll ever write. Next time it will be much easier using the notes you're now developing. Also, some of the material you generate now will not be relevant for THIS resume, but WILL be relevant for your resume later on when your Job Objective changes.

I'd suggest doing the "easy stuff" first, and setting it aside—that is the cut-and-dried Work History and Education & Training. So we'll discuss the process in the following order:

    A.   Work History

    B.   Education & Training

    C.   Job Objective and Skill Areas

        METHOD #1—if you're fairly clear about your Objective:
           Objective . . . what I want to do
           Skill assessment
           —Related Skill areas . . . what skills does THAT require?
           —"One-Liners" . . . proof that I have those skills

        METHOD #2—if you're vague and fuzzy about your Objective:
           Skill Assessment
           —"One-Liners" . . . on my most satisfying work
           —Skill areas . . . what my work demonstrates I'm good at
           Objective . . . something that REQUIRES those favorite skills

    D.   Skill Assessment

        —Writing "One-liners"
        —Arranging One-Liners into Skill Groups
        —Editing & Paring Down

A. Work History

For paid and unpaid jobs or positions, note the dates you started and ended, and record the name and location of the workplace or organization.

Put these in chronological order, and save this as your "Master List."

Later when you rewrite this in final form, look at the sample resumes, such as Deana's on page 31, and also read the TEN TOUGH QUESTIONS, for ideas on
how to minimize gaps in your job history, and
how to account for periods of unemployment.

B. Education & Training

Again, create your Master List, including:
— schools you attended, with dates, degrees, honors;
— personal study in your field—all the classes, workshops, and any other informal ways you have learned;
— any other credentials or certificates.

Later on, edit this Master List; keep the original list intact for future use, and on another sheet of paper, select just those items that will go on this resume because they support your specific job objective.

C. Job Objective & Skill Areas

Compose a clearly stated Job Objective and name the primary Skill Areas that relate to it.

OH SURE! Just like that! Take heart, it is NOT just you. EVERYBODY seems to have a hard time being clear and explicit with their Job Objective. It may be the HARDEST part of the resume to do. But it's also critical to be focused here, if your resume is to be effective.

And LIGHTEN UP ABOUT IT! You're not locking yourself into one role for life . . . you only need to be CLEAR about what you want to do NOW.

Here are two methods:

#1 — if you're clear about your Job Objective
#2 — if you're still vague and fuzzy about your Job Objective

See diagram on page 11.

METHOD #1 First, compose a clearly stated JOB OBJECTIVE. Answer the questions WHAT do I want to do, WHERE do I want to do it, WITH WHOM do I want to do it, AT WHAT LEVEL OF RESPONSIBILITY, and UNDER WHAT SPECIAL CONDITIONS if any?

For example . . .

> WHAT? teacher
> WITH WHOM? teacher of autistic children
> WHERE? in a public school
> LEVEL OF RESPONSIBILITY? head teacher
> CONDITIONS? room for me to be innovative & creative

So, the objective would be, "A POSITION AS HEAD TEACHER OF AUTISTIC CHILDREN IN A PUBLIC SCHOOL WHERE I CAN USE MY SKILLS AS A CREATIVE INNOVATIVE EDUCATOR."

NOTICE how much you can say in one sentence! But you can't say any of this until you're willing to be decisive and clear about what you want to do NOW.

TIPS:

The Job Objective should read word-for-word the same as the employer's job title when you apply for a specific advertised position.

The Job Objective should be expressed in the fewest possible words and should be clear enough to bring up a picture in the reader's mind, seeing you at work.

Method #1 continued

Then, name the SKILL AREAS related to your Job Objective. Generally, two or three Major Skill Areas are adequate for this purpose. (See page 49 for a list of sample Skill Areas.) If you're really familiar with the job or position you're aiming for then naming the Major Skill Areas will be easy. If it's NOT easy, then maybe you need to go back and do a bit of research to see precisely what the job calls for. If there's a published Job Description, read it carefully; you'll find the Skill Areas mentioned in it. Sometimes the D.O.T. (Dictionary of Occupational Titles), at local employment offices and libraries, will have an accurate and detailed description of your desired job.

One way to identify the Skill Areas is to imagine that you're the person doing the hiring.* Ask yourself, "What kind of person do I want for this position? What kind of experience and training am I looking for in the new employee? What skills and expertise do I want?"

EXAMPLE: For the job objective used in our example, "head teacher of autistic children," the Major Skill Areas might be:

A.   TEACHING
B.   ADMINISTRATION
C.   SPECIAL CURRICULUM DEVELOPMENT

EXAMPLE: Martha's job objective (page 21) was "Active administrative role in health care and education, with emphasis in community relations."

And the Major Skill Areas she chose were:

A.   COMMUNITY RELATIONS AND TRAINING
B.   SUPERVISION AND ADMINISTRATION
C.   COUNSELING AND INTERVIEWING

EXAMPLE: Yosi's job objective was "A position in mechanical engineering at the level of Project Engineer responsibility."

He chose the Major Skill Areas of:

A.   SYSTEMS DESIGN
B.   INSPECTION AND MAINTENANCE
C.   COMMUNICATION

*Carry this idea even further, career development counselor Carlene Cole suggests, and WRITE A WANT AD as though you were the employer. Exactly what would the ad say? (Go ahead, WRITE it!)

Method #2   If you're Vague-and-Fuzzy about your Job Objective, don't despair! You can still focus in on an objective by working your way back to it. Go directly to the SKILL ASSESSMENT summarized below and described in detail on the following pages.

Just keep in mind that the Skill Assessment instructions were written with Method #1 in mind — where you know your Job Objective and have identified what Skill Areas relate to it. So instead of labeling each "One-Liner" with an already-identified Skill Area, you'll simply label each with a skill that's reflected. It will all come out in the wash! Hang in there!

a)   Write "One-Liners" — short, descriptive statements describing your most satisfying work experiences*, each statement beginning with an action verb.

See page 12 for how to write One-Liners.
Use the work sheets at the back of this book for organizing them.

b)   Tag each One-Liner with the name of a skill(s) it reflects.

Examples:

"Designed and implemented unique programs and classes"   *Program Development*

"Taught effectively in three different classrooms"   *Teaching*

"Supervised & evaluated student teachers' plans & techniques"   *Supervision*

c)   Notice what skills show up most often alongside your One-Liners, and group similar skills together until you have two, three or four Major Skill Areas.

d)   Compose a clearly stated Job Objective which . . .
— uses the skills you've identified above, and
— answers the who/what/where questions as in Method #1

---

*IMPORTANT!!   Remember, "work" includes anything useful and productive you've ever done — paid or not — regardless of job titles or roles!

Another valuable tool for arriving at your current Job Objective is Richard Bolles' QUICK JOB-HUNTING MAP, included in WHAT COLOR IS YOUR PARACHUTE? and also available at bookstores as a separate work book. Takes time, but it's worth it.

Two Approaches
To Writing Your Resume

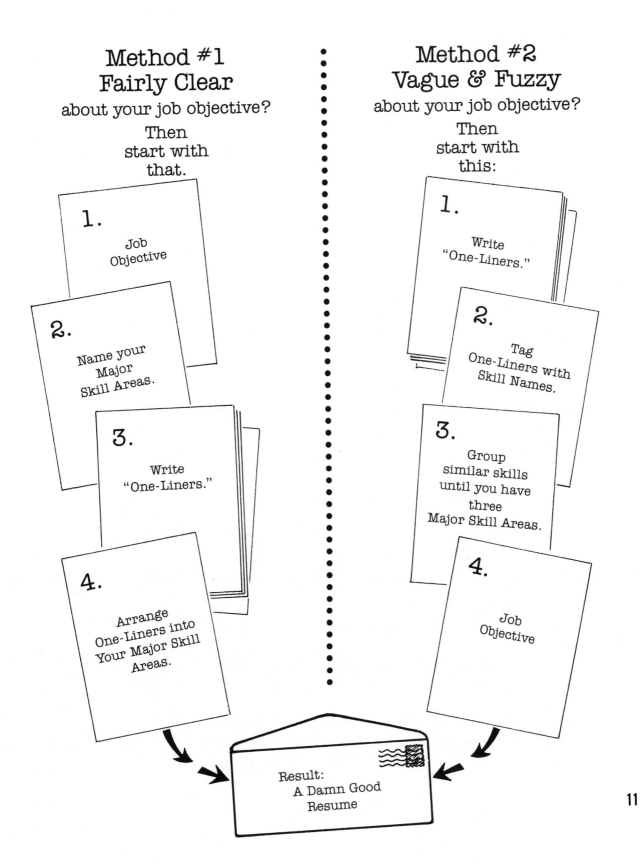

Method #1
Fairly Clear
about your job objective?

Then
start with
that.

1. Job Objective

2. Name your Major Skill Areas.

3. Write "One-Liners."

4. Arrange One-Liners into Your Major Skill Areas.

Method #2
Vague & Fuzzy
about your job objective?

Then
start with
this:

1. Write "One-Liners."

2. Tag One-Liners with Skill Names.

3. Group similar skills until you have three Major Skill Areas.

4. Job Objective

Result:
A Damn Good
Resume

D. Skill Assessment

The Skill Assessment is the HEART of the resume!

You do this in three parts:

1. Writing "One-Liners" describing your experience.
2. Arranging the One-Liners into SKILL GROUPS . . . the same Major Skill Areas that you identified as directly relevant to your Job Objective (clever, eh?).
3. Editing & paring down to final form.
    Work sheets in the back will make this easier.

1. WRITING ONE-LINERS. This is a "brain-storming," where you take each job or volunteer position or work experience, and describe what you actually did, or accomplished, in short One-Liners that begin with action verbs.
    Examples of ONE-LINERS from Dee Ann's resume are on page 20.
    Examples of ACTION VERBS are on page 50.

Just start writing, writing, writing — pouring out the One-Liners that describe your work experience in graphic explicitness. In this process the trick is to CREATE PICTURES IN THE READER'S MIND. Don't be general or vague.

What we want here is a LONG list of SHORT sentences, One-Liners describing all the things you've done, on the job, as a volunteer, in organizations — any way that you have acquired "know-how," skills, abilities, experience, achievements.

Use ACTION WORDS to describe just exactly what you did. Get out your old job descriptions from past employment, if these are available. But don't stop there; you undoubtedly did a lot MORE than all that. Be concrete and specific; do NOT generalize.

IS IT HARD TO GET STARTED?
    Then try this: Think about a typical work day, and describe the actions you took throughout the day: "Contacted agencies for more details, consulted with the boss on strategy, reviewed the records on how they handled this last year" . . . That will get you into the right frame of mind for concreteness in describing what you actually DID: "Designed logo for promotional brochure," "advised clients on housing resources in the area," "wrote annual report to the Board of Directors," "tested the components for reliability of performance" . . . these are specific actions AND create mental pictures. GOT IT?

Take every job or experience that feels at all relevant, and break it down in that way, into the many day-to-day activities you performed. Generate LOTS of material to work with. If in doubt, INCLUDE it. This becomes your MASTER LIST of "One-Liners."

2. ARRANGING THE ONE-LINERS INTO SKILL GROUPS. An easy way to do this is first to assign a letter... "A," "B," "C" to each of the Major Skill Areas that you identified as relevant to your Job Objective.

>EXAMPLE FROM DEE ANN'S RESUME, page 20.
>
>Her Major Skill Areas were:
>A. Business Management
>B. Personnel, Supervision, Training
>C. Food Handling, Preparation & Presentation

Next, look over your list of One-Liners and begin grouping them into Skill Areas this way: read each one and decide which Skill Area you named is most closely related to it, and put the corresponding letter "A," "B," "C" alongside it.

>Again, from Dee Ann's resume, the One-Liners from ONE of her jobs (Co-manager of a coffee-shop/lounge) included these:
>
>— Supervised and trained waitresses and bartenders *B*
>— Ordered food and liquor supplies *C*
>— Prepared payroll and did bookkeeping *A*
>— Decorated the restaurant *A*
>— Planned menus *C*
>— Interviewed, hired and terminated staff *B*
>— Personally greeted foreigners and tourists *A*

So Dee Ann went back and tagged each One-Liner* with the related "A," "B," "C" to show which Major Skill Area was reflected.

Finally, rewrite the list of One-Liners with all the "A"s together, "B"s together, and so forth.

---

*Very often there's an overlap, and a One-Liner will fit in more than one Skill Area... so you just have to PICK ONE! Maybe your experience in one Skill Area is a bit "thinner" than in another, so throw the overlapping ones in that direction.

3. EDITING & PARING DOWN TO FINAL FORM. Now, if you've done it right, you have way too much material for your final resume! Don't fret; save your notes, and on yet another piece of paper begin to pull together similar experiences into single One-Liner statements.

> Examples: "Taught English to fourth graders"
> "Held workshops in grant writing for nonprofit groups"
> "Consulted with student teachers on how to teach
>   special education children"

This becomes, after editing:

> "Taught English to children, grant-writing to adults, and
>   special education techniques to student teachers."

And it fits under your Skill Area labeled "TEACHING."

Keeping your current Job Objective in mind, continue to pare down, combine, eliminate and rephrase each skill group of One-Liners until you have distilled out the BEST wording and the MOST IMPORTANT activities that document your skills.

> SAVE YOUR NOTES! The One-Liners you weed out THIS time
> may fit perfectly on your NEXT resume.

KEY WORDS TO KEEP IN MIND AS
YOU EDIT THE SKILL SECTION:

a) QUANTIFY — Tell HOW MANY, HOW OFTEN, describe tangible products and
      results.

> Examples: "supervised 10 people"
> "produced 24 consecutive issues of a 16-page newsletter"
> "sold a million dollars of real estate the first year as an agent"

b) CREATE PICTURES in the reader's mind — Quantifying is one way (you can SEE
      the 10 people above, and the 16-page newsletter and the million dollars).
      Being very explicit is another; avoid vagueness. Generalizations do NOT
      create mental pictures and so they don't "register" with the reader.

c) BE "PUNCHY" — Say "human relations" instead of "interpersonal relations"
      for example. In-ter-per-son-al is FIVE syllables, while Hu-man is only TWO
      — punchier!

d) REFLECT LEVEL OF RESPONSIBILITY — Employers are looking for evidence of how much responsibility you assumed in jobs you're describing. "Was responsible for" does NOT explain enough. Be explicit:

- "Initiated and wrote a petition signed by 1300 residents to ban nonreturnable bottles, successfully getting it on the ballot."

- "Handled all phases of successful federal grant application for a drop-out project."

- "Taught computer programming to high school students."

- "Interviewed, hired and trained 24 waitresses & bartenders."

- "Self-published a 62-page manual on how to write effective organizational newsletters."

This is hard work, folks! Now you are a Graduated Editor! Whew!

The Highlights or Summary of Qualifications (optional)

*On the following pages are guidelines for writing an effective Summary to go directly beneath your Objective. And the resumes on pages 37 to 48 provide some well written examples (but remember, **don't** copy anything word-for-word).*

This is a good time to decide whether you have room for this section and whether you want to include it. (I strongly recommend it in most cases.)

The Highlights or Summary of Qualifications

"THIS IS WHO I AM, THIS IS WHAT I WANT TO DO,
THIS IS WHY YOU SHOULD HIRE ME TO DO IT."

This section (immediately following your Job Objective) is optional … but, personally I would never omit it from my own resume. Right up front, it presents these two persuasive messages:

1) that you ARE unquestionably qualified, meaning you have the basic skills, credentials and experience (which, alone, is *not* enough to get you the job)
2) *and* that you ALSO are especially talented (even gifted) in areas directly relevant to the job you seek … i.e., that you're "hot."*

And that's a winning combination: basically qualified PLUS unique and special.

All the REST of the resume of course needs to be consistent with the generalizations made in these "highlights," to back them up with facts and figures, to tell How, What, When, Where.

An advantage of using the HIGHLIGHTS section is that you can MAKE SURE the reader gets the essential points you're presenting. Then the Name/Address, Objective, and Highlights—all by themselves—constitute a "mini resume"; if THAT MUCH captures the attention of the reader, they will be willing to read on for the details of your skills and experience.

*(Now I can hear some of you muttering, "Oh, but I'm not sure I'm *really* "hot." In which case you've almost certainly got the *wrong objective,* and then of *course* you wouldn't be hot at *that!* So look again at what you're really "hot" at, what gives you satisfaction and a sense of worth and joy and accomplishment, and reconsider your Objective accordingly.)

How *do* you write a good qualifications summary? (Or "How to Write a 14-line Mini Resume")

Simple; first just imagine this scene:

A real good friend of yours, who knows you very well and knows just what your strengths and special qualities are, JUST HAPPENS to also be professionally acquainted with the Hiring Person at the firm where you'd like to work! Your Good Friend sincerely thinks you'd be just perfect for the Employer's job opening. They are having lunch, and your Good Friend says to the Employer: "Listen, I know the very person for that job; you'd be *crazy* not to hire her. She's got everything you're looking for." And your Good Friend rattles off five hard-hitting, true, appreciative statements about you. These describe your qualifications and strengths so succinctly and persuasively that the Employer is most impressed, and responds with "Well, *sure*, I want to meet her, sounds good to me!"

NOW, *what were* those five hard-hitting, true, appreciative statements your best friend put forth? Whatever they were, *that's* what should be in your Qualifications Summary. It looks so good, and is so direct and relevant and comprehensive, that a Mini Resume is created by the combination of Your Name, Your Objective, and Your Qualifications Summary (or Highlights).

Experiment to illustrate this: take your hand and cover up everything on page 21 (Martha's resume) below the Summary of Qualifications. Those upper few lines constitute a Mini Resume; they say, *"This is who I am, This is what I want to do, This is why you should hire me to do it."* That's really all the employer needs to see, to get excited about this candidate. You can repeat this experiment with Susan's resume on page 48; her name, her objective and her Summary pretty much tell the whole story in a nutshell. Got it?

Look at the Summaries on the resumes in this book for ideas. A typical Summary might include:

> —how much professional experience you have
> —what your formal training and credentials are, if relevant
> —one significant accomplishment, very briefly stated
> —one or two outstanding qualities or skills
> —a reference to your personal values or philosophy, if appropriate

However, **please do not copy someone else's "Highlights"** verbatim! It will not do you justice. Even if everything they say about themselves is also true about you, **that's not the point!** Those are the most important highlights for THAT person for THAT objective, and there's no way this can be identical for YOU with YOUR particular objective.

Finally: Putting It All Together!

ROUGH DRAFT

Assemble the four parts of your resume—job objective, skills presentation, work history, education—and type up a draft copy. Keep it to one page if you can. If your resume MUST be two pages, present your "aces" on page one (objective and skills) and use page two for the back-up documentation (education and work history).

Show this draft to your family and friends and ask them how it "feels." Ask for ideas on improving the wording or layout.

THINGS TO OMIT: Notice what's NOT in the sample resumes here: anything personal and unrelated to the job: age, marital status, height/weight, irrelevant hobbies. Don't include these because they can only create reasons for your resume to be screened OUT, possibly on the basis of just one person's prejudice.

Omit references to jobs that create an image you don't want to take with you. A resume is NOT a "confessional"! It's your document designed expressly to present you in the most favorable light.

CREATIVE EXPRESSION: On Deana's resume, notice how wonderfully "family management" expresses her long-term commitment in this role. The point is, however you chose to spend your time reflects your values, and there is a way to express those values with both honesty and dignity. BUT you may need to be creative with words in order to bypass some people's value prejudices.

FINAL COPY

Look over the sample resumes in this book for format or layout ideas. Martha's is a good example of the minimum amount of white space you need; if your resume is too crowded, it will turn off the reader and it won't work to your benefit. Employers say they'd rather see two pages than one that's overcrowded.

TYPING: Get it typed on the very best typewriter, even if you have to hire somebody to do it for you; it's worth it.

COPIES: Get it copied by the best process; KODAK and XEROX 9500 machines both give excellent results (matte, not shiny) and are cheap. Copies are now so good that you almost can't tell them from the original. Use white or cream-colored paper.

26 Sample Resumes

The following are real resumes of people with whom the author has worked; nothing is "made up," although names and details have been changed to protect people's privacy.

These sample resumes are all produced in one of two ways:

— **typed** on an IBM Selectric typewriter in "Letter Gothic" typestyle, chosen for its readability, appearance and compactness.

— **word-processed** on an Apple MACINTOSH computer (MacWrite software) in "Geneva" font, chosen for the same reasons as above.

Word processed resumes have become commonplace and offer a great advantage: they're a cinch to revise and update frequently, at minimal cost. (The author discourages type-set resumes.)

DEE ANN JACKSON
94 Majestic Drive N.
Santa Barbara, CA
567-7890

Special tip - This layout was a favorite with employers who reviewed the resumes.

OBJECTIVE: Position as Assistant Manager Trainee in a restaurant

RESTAURANT EXPERIENCE

Business Management

* Prepared payroll for staff of 10; light bookkeeping
* Opened and closed cash registers, and made bank deposits
* Wrote all correspondence and maintained records for taxes
* Personally greeted foreigners and tourists
* Decorated & cleaned restaurant; arranged for equipment maintenance

Personnel, Supervision, Training

* Supervised and taught 15 waitresses and 4 bartenders
* Mediated employee relationships to maintain cooperative working atmosphere
* Interviewed, hired and terminated staff
* Successfully taught very inexperienced people to deal effectively with the public

Food Handling, Preparation and Presentation

* Ordered food and liquor supplies, organized stockroom, maintained inventory
* Monitored orderliness and cleanliness in preparation areas and especially in publicly visible food preparation areas
* Planned menus, did comparative food shopping, oversaw quality and accuracy of deliveries
* Supervised the preparation, arrangement and serving of food

WORK HISTORY

1983-85   OWNER, CO-MANAGER - Coffee Roy's Inc. Coffee Shop/Lounge - San Jose CA

1972-82   ASSISTANT MANAGER - Willetts Livestock, Inc. - horse auction co, Arkansas
* Catalogued livestock, settled sales between buyers and sellers; published monthly newsletter for customers, managed 3-person office

1970-71   ADMINISTRATIVE ASSISTANT - Fort Marks Fire Dept. - Fort Marks, Arkansas
* Prepared payroll for staff of 118, made appointments, wrote correspondence

EDUCATION

1968-70   Fort Marks Junior College - Arkansas

MARTHA T. SAWYER
1914 Derby Ave.
Walnut Creek, CA
(415) 441-2633

OBJECTIVE

Active administrative role in health care and
education, with emphasis on community relations

SUMMARY OF QUALIFICATIONS

* Over 10 years experience in varied human relations responsibilities.
* Graduate degree in the social sciences, with fieldwork training in
  medical and psychiatric settings.
* Well developed communication and assessment skills.
* Ability to work independently and with multidisciplinary team.
* Experience in program presentation and group facilitation.

PROFESSIONAL EXPERIENCE

Community Relations and Training

* Served as agency liaison to high school and college classes; guest lecturer
  on health and welfare issues.
* Recruited adoptive parents for hard-to-place children. Organized and
  coordinated training sessions and support groups.
* Presented program and services briefings.
* Graduated from and facilitated stop smoking groups.

Supervision and Administration

* Coordinated in-house and inter-agency case planning on extended medical
  care and adoptions.
* Learned the budgetary intricacies of public assistance; supervised 10 technicians; authorized disbursements of thousands of dollars monthly.
* Prepared comprehensive reports and recommendations for agency and court use.

Counseling and Interviewing

* Crisis intervention and long term counseling with individuals and families
  of diverse backgrounds and status, dealing with stress of illness and
  disability, and life transitions.
* Investigative interviewing; in-depth personal assessments.

EMPLOYMENT HISTORY

Current	Kaiser Hospitals, Richmond, CA
	Medical Social Worker
1977-1984	Alameda County Human Resources Agency, Oakland, CA
	Adoption Counselor; Investigator--child abuse
1976-1977	San Francisco Social Services Department
	Supervisor, Income Maintenance

EDUCATION

BA cum laude	Sociology - Barret College, Michigan
MSW	University of Michigan

SUZY L. CRANE
1970 Yorkshire Road W.
Oakland, CA 94602
(415) 711-5430

OBJECTIVE: Storyteller for Deaf Children for the
California Arts Council's Artists in Residence Program

PROFESSIONAL EXPERIENCE

Storytelling / Theatre

* Told stories in American Sign Language to over 100 children in 14 classrooms at the California School for the Deaf, funded by California Arts Council.

* Established the initial phases of a storytelling video library for the California School for the Deaf and for the San Francisco Public Library.

* Developed theatre pieces in Sign Language as a member of a group of deaf and hearing artists.

* Performed stories for deaf children and Sign Language students at the San Francisco Public Library.

* Selected and told stories to elementary school hearing children.

* Introduced classroom storytelling to Costa Rican deaf children, using American/Spanish Sign Language.

Sign Language

* Interpreted for two deaf teenagers in a mainstreaming program.

* Interpreted for college level courses in psychology, deaf culture, biology, auto mechanics, and horsemanship.

* Interpreted for deaf professionals in business transactions and meetings.

* Lived and worked in a summer camp for the deaf; I was the only hearing person among 50 staff members and campers.

Teaching

* Assisted individual deaf children in their classroom work in math, language, and reading, as a teachers' aide.

* Taught second and fifth grade elementary school children in both public and private school settings.

* Tutored two deaf high-school students in English, Algebra and Social Studies.

* Developed and supervised arts and sports activities for deaf and multiply-handicapped youngsters.

EMPLOYMENT HISTORY

Current   <u>Sign Language Interpreter/Tutor</u> - Las Lomas High School, Walnut Creek CA

1985   <u>Administrative/Production Assistant</u> - RAINBOW'S END, Educational television program for deaf children, Project of D.E.A.F. Media, INC., Emeryville CA

Co-creator of Bay Area Sign Language Theatre, Oakland CA

1984-85   <u>Consultant/Storyteller</u> - Mima Brava Association, Costa Rica, Central America

1983-84   <u>Storyteller</u> - California School for the Deaf, Berkeley; and San Francisco Public Library

1981-83   <u>Sign Language Interpreter</u> - University of Massachusetts, Amherst MA; and DCARA (Deaf Counseling, Advocacy & Referral Agency), Oakland CA

Summer 1982   <u>Senior Counselor</u> - Friends of the Deaf Summer Camp, Glen Ellen CA

1982   <u>Teacher's Aide</u> - California School for the Deaf, Berkeley CA

1981-82   <u>Student Teacher</u> - Jackson Street Elementary School, and Smith College Alternative School, Northampton MA

EDUCATION & SPECIALIZED TRAINING

B.A., Hampshire College, Amherst MA - 1983

Voice to Sign - Vista College, Berkeley CA - 1986

Studied with professional deaf performers in television production in San Francisco CA - 1985

Advanced American Sign Language - Center for Independent Living, Berkeley CA - 1982

Creative Uses of American Sign Language - Ohlone College, Fremont CA - 1981

CERTIFICATION

Massachusetts Elementary Teaching Certificate

MARGARET ROBERTS
333 Cityview Highway
Oakland, CA 94606
655-9941

OBJECTIVE
System Assistant in College Hire Program

← Note—This is the actual employer's job-title

PROFESSIONAL SKILLS

PROGRAM DEVELOPMENT

* Designed and implemented unique programs and classes, such as Practical English for non-college-bound seniors, and Community Career Project for Junior High students.

* Developed successful campaign for sole bargaining, resulting in my organization being chosen to represent teachers in negotiations with school board.

COMMUNICATION

* Handled grievances at informal and formal levels for Title IX non-compliance. (Title IX refers to federal law dealing with sexism in schools)

* Authored and co-authored:
    60-page labor contract
    Five newspaper articles informing community of Title IX law
    Extensive year-end reports as committee chair
    Procedures, forms, grants guidelines for innovative programs

* Team-taught effectively in three different classrooms.

ANALYSIS AND EVALUATION

* As freelance tutor, diagnosed individual learning needs.

* Supervised and evaluated student teachers' plans and techniques.

* Surveyed District and reported on in-service needs for continuing education programs.

* Oversaw District actions to assure compliance with federal guidelines on sexism.

COORDINATION AND SUPERVISION

* Handled all phases of successful federal grant application.

* Organized and supervised all aspects of 6-week summer school, including hiring, ordering supplies, developing course offerings.

* Chaired professional negotiations for unit of 550 teachers.

* Initiated a petition signed by 1300 residents to ban non-returnable bottles & cans.

EMPLOYMENT HISTORY

1977 - present   Middle School Teacher
                  Mill Valley Elementary School, Mill Valley, CA

1980 - present   Tutor, freelance (ages 7-44)

1972 - 1977   Elementary School Teacher
                  Mill Valley Elementary School, Mill Valley, CA

1969 - 1972   English Teacher (grades 10-12)
                  Lincoln Park High School, Lincoln Park, Michigan

PROFESSIONAL ACTIVITIES

* District Coordinator, Title IX (federal law regarding sexism in schools)
* In-Service Chairperson
* Innovations Committee Chairperson
* Multi-Ethnic Committee; English Curriculum Committee
* Co-Chair for Federal Innovations grants project for potential drop-outs
* Contract Writer, Negotiator, Spokesperson, Vice-President, Chairperson for
    Professional Negotiations, Co-Chairperson Sole Bargaining Election;
    Mill Valley and Lincoln Park Teachers' Associations
* Field Representative Intern, Michigan Education Association

EDUCATION

BA, Park College, 1969 - Parkerville, MO
48 hours post-graduate work: counseling, science, literature, art.

Certification: Michigan Standard Secondary
                California Standard Elementary
                California Standard Secondary

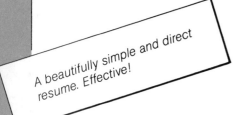

FRANKLIN FELDMANN
1200 Martindale Drive
Oakland, Calif. 94602
(415) 655-8977

JOB OBJECTIVE: Position as Computer Service Manager

SUMMARY OF QUALIFICATIONS

* Skilled in diagnosis and repair
* Familiar with Commodore equipment
* Extensive experience as electronics technician
* Ability to work independently
* Enjoy working with computers

DIAGNOSIS & REPAIR EXPERIENCE

- Found and replaced defective components on PET computers, using Commodore's diagnostic programs.

- Solved problems beyond scope of diagnostic program, such as: located thermal related integrated circuit failure; found unstripped wire in keyboard connector.

- Tested and maintained electronic equipment, including microcomputers, using oscilloscope, voltmeter, signal generator, logic probe, etc.

WORK EXPERIENCE

1967-1985   <u>Senior Electronics Technician</u> - University of California, Berkeley, Radio Astronomy Laboratory
Working with engineers' sketches and diagrams, was responsible for layout, fabrication, testing and installation of sensitive receivers and computer control equipment for radio and optical telescopes.

1964-1966   <u>Product Design Engineer</u> - Eldorado Electronics, Berkeley.
Developed prototypes for high speed electronic counters.

1961-1964   <u>Electronics Technician</u> - Beckman Instruments, Richmond

EDUCATION

Santa Monica City College - engineering major, 2 years
University of California, Berkeley - Electrical Engineering major - 1 year
Currently taking course in machine language programming.

SHARI MILTON
997 Centerfield Road
Berkeley, Calif. 94708
(415) 948-8864

JOB OBJECTIVE

Department Manager trainee for direct sales & customer service
in a quality women's clothing store

SKILLS & EXPERIENCE

SALES & CUSTOMER SERVICE---Demonstrated jewelry and advised customers about style; researched market availability of customer-preferred merchandise.

ORGANIZATION & PLANNING----Organized fashion shows; planned selections of merchandise appropriate to customers' age groups, tastes, and in response to public fashion trends; worked within a budget as assistant buyer.

LEADERSHIP & MANAGEMENT----Coordinated program of Service Club, for fashion, speech, and community activities; acted as President of Girls Club.

EMPLOYMENT HISTORY

Salesperson & Assistant Buyer--Lilly Enterprises: Fine Jewelry & Home Access-
                          ories (family business)   1982-85

Broker's Assistant--Milton & Hesse Insurance Company   1985
                (handled claims, endorsements, and incoming client calls)

Dental Chairside Assistant--Nathan Harbin DDS & Arnold Stein DDS   1983-85

Instructional Aide - Piedmont & Laurel Day Care Centers   summer   1981

AA Degree, Merritt College, 1981; General Education
College of Alameda, Dental Assistant Program, Certificate & License, 1981

27

George and I struggled to get this resume together. But…a couple of weeks later he was able—on his own—to do a second resume geared to a different job objective. (See next page.)

GEORGE RAVEN
775 Delaware Street
Miller Creek CA 94805
415/482-1119

OBJECTIVE: Position as a commercial real estate analyst / mortgage banker leading to top levels of responsibility

PROFESSIONAL SKILLS

Developmental and Promotional

* Initiated contact with public entities interested in financing $10.5 million worth of projects.
* Opened new territory and took applications for $1.7 million conventional, FHA and VA loans and funded $750,000 in the first three months of business.
* Guest lectured on real estate financing at junior college and professional offices.

Analytical

* Consulted with two major San Francisco law firms to write official statement for municipal bond issue.
* In coordination with the City Sanitary District, developed expectations of tax revenues for purposes of bond re-payment.
* Developed mathematical model describing repayment schedule of unique bond issue.

Technical

* Wrote first drafts of $2.5 million bond issue official statement.
* Negotiated for exclusive rights contract to consult and underwrite bond issue.
* Taught computer programming and statistics at the high school level.

Innovative

* Initiated changes in underwriting procedures for first trust deeds to speed funding.
* Initiated procedural changes to streamline loan processing with a limited staff.
* Developed new math courses for gifted high school students.

EMPLOYMENT HISTORY

Loan Officer - Mortgage Banking Services, San Francisco (1984-present)
Financial Consultant - Investment Bankers, Inc., San Francisco (1983-84)
Math Teacher - City Public Schools, Miller Creek CA (1976-83)
Recreation Leader - City Recreation Department, Miller Creek CA (1976-present)

EDUCATION & PROFESSIONAL CREDENTIALS

M.A., Economics, 1982; State University of California. Second major, math, 1978.
Secondary credential, 1977; Junior College credential, 1983.
B.A., Economics, 1974; University of California
Real Estate Brokers License, 1985 - Extension program, Community College.
Over 20 seminars and classes in real estate and finance (see attached list).

GEORGE RAVEN
775 Delaware Street
Miller Creek, CA 94805
415/482-1119

OBJECTIVE: Position as Manager of Development & Promotion
with a professional / recreational sports program

PROFESSIONAL EXPERIENCE

Promotion

* Planned and coordinated a soccer jamboree in conjunction with the City Youth
  Soccer Advisory Board. Participation & attendance broke all past records.
* Organized, coordinated and promoted high school soccer team.
* Promoted a soccer program for adults, obtaining sponsorship from local merchants.

Development

* Original member of City Youth Soccer Advisory Board which developed a city-wide
  program.
* Designed and implemented sailing program for disadvantaged youth.
* Developed, with no funding, a Junior Varsity soccer team at local high school.
* Initiated new business worth over $10 million, in a short period of time, as both
  a financial consultant and as a loan officer.

Management & Organization

* Managed adult softball, basketball and volleyball teams.
* Taught in public schools for 8 years with 150 students per day.
* Coached at junior high school, high school, and junior college levels.

Involvement in Sports

* Little League, Pony League, high school and college baseball.
* Intramural college sports.
* City Adult Recreational League.
* Individual sports: skiing, swimming, tennis, golf, running, surfing, sailing.

EMPLOYMENT HISTORY

Recreation Leader - Parks and Recreation Dept., Miller Creek CA - 1976-present
Coach - Community Junior College; Rockville High School; Morgan High School; Miller
         Creek High School, Kane Junior High School; Youth Soccer Program - 1976-83
Math Teacher - public schools, Miller Creek & Wynforde Hill, CA 1976-83
Loan Officer - Mortgage Banking Services - San Francisco CA - 1984-present
Financial Consultant - Investment Bankers, Inc., San Francisco CA - 1983-84

EDUCATION & PROFESSIONAL CREDENTIALS

M.A., Economics, 1982; State University of California. Second major, math, 1978
                     Secondary credential, 1977; Junior College credential, 1983
B.A., Economics, 1974; University of California
United States Soccer Federation, Coaching License - 1981
United States Red Cross, Sailing Instructor's License - 1979

ROGER M. MARTIN
1899 Delaware St - Apt. 9
Berkeley, CA 94704
848-2355 (home)
849-2573 (work)

OBJECTIVE: Position as STAFF PHARMACIST in a hospital, community or professional pharmacy, offering opportunities for educational and professional advancement.

QUALIFICATIONS

* Thorough knowledge of drug interactions and pharmacology.
* Ability to deal with the public in a professional and concerned manner.
* Facility in consulting with doctors on questions concerning medications.

PHARMACY EXPERIENCE

Community Services

* Prepared and dispensed pharmaceuticals in a community pharmacy for over 3 years.

* Maintained drug inventory dealing both direct and through wholesale.

* Back-up supervisor for staff of 5-6 employees.

Nursing Home Services

* Dispensed pharmaceuticals to 4 nursing homes over a period of 3 years.

* Designed and implemented an in-patient education program for nursing home staff on a monthly basis.

* Reviewed Medication Profiles monthly for 3 nursing homes.

EMPLOYMENT HISTORY

Current   ATTENDANT FOR PHYSICALLY DISABLED, Physically Disabled Students Program, Berkeley, CA
1982-1984 STAFF PHARMACIST, White Cross Pharmacy, Inc., Providence, RI
1980-1982 PHARMACY INTERN, White Cross Pharmacy, Inc., Providence, RI
1981-1982 RESEARCH ASSISTANT, Dept. of Pharmacognosy, University of Rhode Island
1978-1980 RESEARCH ASSISTANT, Environmental Protection Agency, Dept. of Biochemistry, North Kingston, RI
1978   CO-RECREATION DIRECTOR, Presbyterian Home for Children, Farmington, MO
1976-1978 RESEARCH ASSISTANT, Southeastern Massachusetts University, Dept. of Micro-biology, N. Dartmouth, MA

EDUCATION

B.S., Pharmacy - University of Rhode Island, 1978-1982

Biology Major - Southeastern Massachusetts University, 1976-1978

DEANA JUNE DUNNLAP
119 Richards Lane
Berkeley CA 94707
(415) 357-0923

OBJECTIVE: Management trainee position in retail sales, using my skills in design, research, administration and public contact.

PROFESSIONAL EXPERIENCE & SKILLS

Management   Coordinated operations, managed and assisted in sales at Hiller Downtown Bookshop and the End of The World Import & Export Company, Oakland.

Managed small research laboratory at Columbia University.

Trained military personnel in Bacteriological procedures at Sixth Army Medical Laboratory.

Administration   Wrote and catalogued procedures for biology laboratory in Oakland, CA. Designed new record forms, evaluated and carried out daily work priorities.

Coordinated numerous experiments from inception through subsequent interpretation and reporting of findings.

Research   Textile design research completed at the Farmer's Museum, Roper College and museums in Guatemala and Mexico. Written and photographic reports submitted to Design Department, Univ. Nevada.

Design   Designed and constructed loom and non-loom textiles. Exhibited work in California fiber shows.

Display   Planned and installed window and in-store displays of merchandise for Berkeley and San Francisco merchants. Successfully promoted sales.

Special Skills Extensive photographic and dark room experience - 35 mm and 4x5 formats.

WORK HISTORY

1986   Research Assistant - Grovers Cancer Research Institute, Richmond CA
1985   Sales & Operations - End of the World Imports & Exports, Oakland CA
                                    Hiller Downtown Bookshop, San Francisco CA
1982-1985   Graduate School
1964-1982   Family management and independent study
1957-1964   Biological Research Assistant

EDUCATION

M.A., Visual Design - University of Nevada
B.S., Zoology-Bacteriology - New Haven College for Women - New Haven, Conn.

References & Portfolio available on request

31

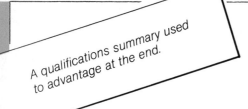
A qualifications summary used to advantage at the end.

VALERIE W. LENZO
333 Marina Ave.
Berkeley, CA 94708
(415) 524-7337

OBJECTIVE: Lecturer on Nursing Law & Ethics in a basic or continuing education nursing program.

RELATED SKILLS

Teaching

* Developed curriculum for continuing and in-service nurses on legal issues.
* Instructed sophomore baccalaureate nursing students in clinical skills.
* Taught infant care and breast-feeding to new mothers.

Research and Drafting

* Analyzed and synthesized medical records for trial preparation.
* Drafted health legislation to increase Medi-Cal benefits.
* Researched history and legislative development of the Calif. Nurse Practice Act.
* Investigated and intervened for constituents having problems with government agencies

Organization and Supervision

* Solicited and scheduled testimony for legislative hearings.
* Organized RNs for labor negotiations, including planning and strategy.
* Supervised new staff nurses; often acted as charge nurse.

EMPLOYMENT HISTORY

1985 to present   Medical-Legal Consultant / Researcher. Self-employed, working with attorneys in private practice.
1980 - 1986   Registered Nurse. Alta Bates Hospital, Berkeley, CA
1983 - 1985   Legislative Intern. Assembly member Thomas Bates, Oakland, CA
1982 - 1983   Law Clerk. McKinley & Seward, San Francisco, CA

EDUCATION, LICENSURE, AFFILIATIONS

J.D. - University of California School of Law, 1985. Admitted California Bar, 12/85
B.S. - Summa Cum Laude, State Univ. of Georgia, School of Nursing
       Licensed California Registered Nurse, 11/80
Member: Calif. Nurses Assoc.; American Nurses Assoc.; National Lawyers Guild

SUMMARY OF QUALIFICATIONS

Working knowledge of the structure and functions of the health care system; years of experience as a registered nurse.

Understanding of Labor Law, grievance handling, and negotiation process; ability to convey complex concepts in understandable terms.

Experience in analyzing medical records and identifying legal issues in complex cases.

JENNIFER SWEET, MSW, LCSW
3400 Sixteenth Street
San Francisco, CA
(415) 641-4666

OBJECTIVE: Senior or supervisory MEDICAL SOCIAL WORK position in an acute care hospital or outpatient clinic related to a hospital

PROFESSIONAL EXPERIENCE

Administration & Supervision

* Supervised and/or trained graduate students, outreach workers and therapists.
* Served as Acting Director of acute care hospital social service department.
* Designed documentation and evaluation procedures for accreditation.
* Interviewed personnel, facilitated meetings, mediated conflicts.
* Organized parent participation to develop a day care center.

Cross-Cultural Skills

* Bi-lingual in English and Spanish.
* Lived and worked with people of various cultures and social strata.
* Provided services to clientele of multi-ethnic community.
* Did independent study in 8 South American countries.

Counseling and Interviewing

* Conducted long & short-term psychotherapy for 10 years, with individuals and families.
* Specialized in teaching & facilitating women's problem-solving groups.
* Provided crisis intervention in several units of acute care hospital.
* Acted as patient interpreter, advocate and outreach counselor.
* Performed investigative interviews and diagnostic evaluations.

EMPLOYMENT HISTORY

1983-now	Acting Director of Medical Social Work - ST. LUKE'S HOSPITAL, San Francisco
1980-1983	Psychotherapist - FORT HELP, San Francisco
1981-1982	Psychotherapist - CITY COLLEGE OF SAN FRANCISCO, Mental Health Program
1980-1981	Teaching Assistant - FREDERICK BURK ELEMENTARY SCHOOL, San Francisco
1977-1978	Social Worker - MISSION CHILDCARE CONSORTIUM, San Francisco
1975-1977	Medical Social Worker - MISSION NEIGHBORHOOD HEALTH CENTER, San Francisco

EDUCATION

Clinical Social Work License #777, State of California
MSW University of California, Berkeley. Community Mental Health
    National Institute of Mental Health Award, 1977.

PROFESSIONAL AFFILIATION: Member, Bay Area Assoc. of Spanish Speaking Therapists.
PUBLICATION: 1974. Co-authored Journey Through the Clouds: 8 Days on the Inca Trail.

KARL SINGER
378 Eshelman Avenue
Berkeley CA 94703
(415) 939-7255

JOB OBJECTIVE: Position as Field Service Representative
with National Software Corporation

PROFESSIONAL EXPERIENCE

Technical Expertise

* Repaired and maintained a wide range of equipment including: mainframes, minicomputers, microcomputers, hard disk units, floppy disk units, data terminals, letter quality printers, dot matrix printers, line printers, teletype printers (KSR), electronic cash registers, modems (Bell-type 202,212 and ALD's) and mag tape units.

* Conducted numerous pre-installation surveys, recommended electrical and cooling system modifications, and supervised installation of computer systems.

* Utilized remote and on-site diagnostics. Familiar with use of oscilloscopes, data scopes, volt ohm meters, EIA breakout boxes and other types of test equipment.

* Studied machine level codes and assembler language to enhance troubleshooting skills.

Administration & Management

* Designed a better maintenance form, resulting in more timely billing and a simplified form for data entry to project future maintenance cost and profits.

* Successfully negotiated a subdealership with a Commodore computer dealer, adding valuable training and parts access to the capabilities of our maintenance department.

* Established a field service department: hired technicians, created forms, established contacts with manufacturers for parts and some board repairs, stocked tool kits, ordered special tools, established service policies, set up and maintained spare parts inventory, developed maintenance schedules, handled customer relations.

* Supervised a major overhaul project (one year) of the central shipboard tactical data system, reworking and repairing all computers and peripheral equipment.

* Succeeded in complex teamwork with other shipboard supervisors to assure that equipment and system repairs and testings were coordinated and completed on time to meet scheduled interface testing requirements.

EMPLOYMENT HISTORY

1985 - present	Field Service Manager - Coast Computer Systems Inc., Oakland CA
1984 - 1985	Field Engineer - National Cash Register, San Francisco CA
1983 - 1984	Customer Engineer - Control Data Corporation, Berkeley CA
1977 - 1983	Data Systems Technician - United States Navy

(continued)

34

EDUCATION & SPECIALIZED TRAINING

Chapman College - Orange CA.   **Math** - 1982
Long Beach Community College - Long Beach CA.   General - 1981

Xerox Corporation, Hayward CA.   Diablo Letter-Quality Printers - 1986

Digital Microsystems, Oakland CA.   DMS **Computers** - 1986

National Cash Register, Dayton OH.   NCR 2140 Point of Sale System - 1984

Control Data Corporation, Minneapolis MN.   CDC Cyber 170 Computer System and associated **peripherals** - 1983

United States Navy.   Data System Technician Basic "A" and "C" School - 1977-79

PHIL MILLER
1224 Wilson Boulevard
San Francisco CA 94131
(415) 229-1100

OBJECTIVE: Position as outside sales representative

HIGHLIGHTS OF EXPERIENCE

* In 1982, was second in the nation in quarterly commission sales of audio accessories at Quickmart Distribution.

* Represented my company to upper management of major retailers such as Sears, Montgomery Wards, PayLess, Woolworth, Tower Records.

* Earned commendation from Division Manager for effectively handling complete set-up of a new record/tapes department for established customer.

PROFESSIONAL QUALIFICATIONS

Creative Promotion

* Set up dozens of effective displays capturing product excitement to promote sales.

* Earned prize for creative display in contest to promote record sales.

* Assessed the likely demand for prerecorded country-western music in a rural-based retail store, resulting in exceptionally high record sales.

Professional Salesmanship

* Established and maintained consistent schedule for servicing accounts and built up a sense of trust and dependability.

* Successfully applied in saleswork the acute listening skills developed over 3 years as a paraprofessional counselor (volunteering at Berkeley Free Clinic).

* Re-established customer trust on accounts that had been previously under-serviced.

Administration & Management

* Managed a retail music center, including opening and closing, ordering merchandise from sales reps, and supervising a small sales staff.

* Prepared timely reports on sales volume, inventory and budget forecasts.

* Covered entire Northern California sales area and worked effectively with minimal supervision.

EMPLOYMENT

1985-now   Sales Representative, QUICKMART DISTRIBUTION CO, Rack Services Division; San Francisco, CA

1985   Manager (re-hired, promoted) TOWN & COUNTRY MUSIC CENTER, San Diego, CA
1984*   Asst. Manager/Salesperson   TOWN & COUNTRY MUSIC CENTER, San Diego, CA
           (* left for school; returned 1985, promoted to manager)

1982-1983 Salesperson, MIRAVISTA MUSIC CENTER, Daly City, CA

EDUCATION

College of the Redwoods, Eureka, CA - 1984/85

ESTELLE GADE
9843 Thirty-second Avenue
Oakland, CA 94605
415-614-2020

Estelle is still in high school, and will be working part time until graduation; she shows the relevance of her work at Mac-Donald's.

Current objective: Part time entry level position in Bookkeeping
1986 Objective: Full time Bookkeeping position after high school graduation

HIGHLIGHTS OF QUALIFICATIONS

- Earned an Outstanding Achievement raise at MacDonald's.
- Excellent at thinking through problem situations.
- Completed Accounting and Law classes with high grades.
- Get along with people well; fine communication skills.
- 1 year successful experience in Bookkeeping & Cashiering at MacDonald's.

EXPERIENCE

Bookkeeping
* Accurately completed bookkeeping tasks at MacDonald's in half the usual time required.
* Recorded daily sales
   - tallied total items sold and computed total daily revenues
   - recorded totals of wasted food and paper products
   - audited the cash-register records for each employee, and produced a monthy report
     showing where cashiering errors occurred.
* Earned an Outstanding Achievement raise at MacDonald's for consistently accurate money
  handling and good relationships with customers.
* Assisted in computing employee hours on time cards and verifying accuracy of vendor statements.
* Balanced family checkbook statements and paid bills.

Administrative Assistance
* Assisted store manager in orienting and assigning employees
   - prepared new employee personnel folders
   - called substitutes to fill in during illness or rush hours.
* Monitored minors' work permits to assure they were still valid.
* Filed personnel records and manager's test results.
* Posted and filed official documents.
* Typed correspondence; answered telephone; scheduled interviews; made reservations.

WORK HISTORY

1985	Fulltime student	Skyline High School – Oakland
Nov.84–Apr.85	Bookkeeper	MAC DONALD'S – Oakland
Oct.83 –Nov.84	Cashier	MAC DONALD'S – Oakland and Hayward
summer 1983	Clerk	HAVENSCOURT COMMUNITY CHURCH – Oakland
weekends 1981	Cashier/sales asst.	CERAMIC TILE CO. – Oakland

EDUCATION & TRAINING
Senior – Skyline High School, Oakland
Business courses: Accounting, Law, Typing, Journalism
President of student union organization   -   Co-editor of student newspaper

MICHEAL BLACKWOOD
1213 Hearst St.
Santa Cruz CA
(408) 229-1914

Objective: position as project director, in non-profit housing development

SUMMARY OF QUALIFICATIONS

- 11 years involvement with administration of non-profit housing
- Served on Board of Directors of two housing coops
- Served on planning commission of a major intentional community
- Managed or directed:
  - manufacturing business grossing $250,000/year
  - workforce of 60
  - residential community
  - environmental bookstore & business office

PROFESSIONAL EXPERIENCE

Project Management
* Served as Personnel Manager, overseeing all laborforce issues, including:
  - matching invidividual preferences & work requisitions
  - designing and maintaining work-hours accounting system
  - planning & projecting labor flow
  - counseling workers on career development and training options
  - mediating conflicts among workers and managers
  - preparing budget proposals & presenting them for membership approval
* Set up books and annual budget & process at Walnut House Coop.
* Appointed & trained management committees, and monitored their progress.

Initiative & Innovation
* Started a worker-owned business and served as its first manager.
* Designed & implemented a comprehensive process of long-term resource and social planning for a residential community of 60 people.
* Helped organize an urban Limited Equity Housing Coop conversion.

Non-Profit Housing
* Personally lived in cooperative housing for the last eleven years.
* Trained in getting DRE subdivision approval.
* Familiar with the complexities of developing Limited Equity Housing Cooperatives.
* Knowledgeable in financial management of non-profit housing.
* Trained shared-housing participants in:
  - communication skills
  - conflict resolution/mediation
  - personal needs assessment
  - cooperative assertiveness
  - organizing & facilitating meetings
  - bookkeeping & financial planning

EMPLOYMENT HISTORY

1980-1984	Office Manager/Bookstore Manager	THE ECOLOGY CENTER - Berkeley CA
1974-1979	Director, Personnel Manager & Planning Commissioner	EAST WIND COMMUNITY, INC. - Tecumseh MO

38

DAVID QUINLAN
902 Alcatraz
Oakland CA
653-8762

Current Job Objective: a position as electronics assembler
(Future goal: Electronics Technician)

QUALIFICATIONS & EXPERIENCE

* Very strong interest in electronics; I spend much of my spare time on:
    - reading and studying electronics (Popular Electronics and many books on the subject)
    - redesigning circuitry, replacing components, servicing, alignment of tuned circuits in radios, assembly and disassembly.
* Experience rebuilding and repairing:
    - tape recorders
    - stereo receiver
    - one TV
    - car radios
* Technical skills:
    - soldering
    - component identification (color coding)
    - reading schematics
    - using test equipment (oscilloscope, voltmeters, signal generators)
* Studied Electronics theory and Radio/TV Repair at community colleges.

EMPLOYMENT HISTORY

1982-85	Freelance auto mechanics and electronics repair
4/83-11/84	Assembler & driver – Spring Mountain Hot Tubs, Berkeley CA
3/82-2/83	Farm worker – Battlebrook Farm (family farm) – Bancroft ME
10/81-5/82	Fountain person – Kramer's Ice Cream, Berkeley CA
1979-82	Newspaper routeman – San Francisco Chronicle (while in school)

EDUCATION

Laney College – TV and Radio Repair – one semester, Fall 1983
Merritt College – Electronics Theory – three semesters 1981 & 1985
Berkeley High School & Berkeley Adult School – Equivalency certificate 1984

SUZANNE POOLE

Campus Address:
3022 Haste St., Apt. 267
Berkeley, CA 94705
(415) 832-6743

Alternate Address:
6290 Marin Court
Concord, CA 94521
(415) 677-0905

Objective: entry level position in Audit Department

HIGHLIGHTS OF QUALIFICATIONS

- Dedicated to professionalism, highly motivated toward goal achievment.
- Successful in mastering accounting theory and technical skills.
- 3 years demonstrated effectiveness in interpersonal communications.
- Experience in coordinating projects involving people and activities.

EDUCATION & TRAINING

B.S., Accounting – University of California, Berkeley – May 1986
Honor student since Fall semester 1983 ● Accounting G.P.A. 4.0 – Overall G.P.A. 3.685

AFFILIATIONS

U.C. Berkeley Honor Society – Professional Women's Assoc. – Undergraduate Business Assoc.

EXPERIENCE & SKILLS

Technical and Business Knowledge

* Developed solid theoretical grounding in financial accounting; able to set up balance sheets and income statements, and analyze clients' assets and liabilities.
* Studied laws relevant to accounting and other business applications.
* Edited market research interviews; entered coded data into computer and generated reports.

Leadership/Coordination

* Developed the confidence of owners of market research firm, and was invited to assume more responsibility through a supervisory position.
* Coordinated focus group studies for a market research firm, involving phone invitations to prospective group members & providing refreshments and study materials.
* Organized participation in a soccer team: contacted prospective players and got commitment to participate; maintained attendance records, statistics at games, and medical/equipment inventory.

Communications and Interpersonal Skills

* Successfully persuaded shoppers to volunteer time for in-person market research interviews.
* Solicited phone interviews from random samples, consistently convincing participants of the legitimacy and value of the project and the importance of their opinions.
* Gave oral reports and evaluations on market research interviews, to clients from ad agencies.
* Collaborated with co-workers to assure consistent coding of research materials.
* Assist students with their problems in accounting classes, and grade homework (current job).

WORK HISTORY

1985 fall	Reader	UC BERKELEY BUSINESS SCHOOL – Berkeley CA
1984 summer	Sales Clerk	SHOE TOWN – Concord CA
June'83-Aug'84	Interviewer	QED MARKETING RESEARCH – Walnut Creek CA
Apr'81-Mar'83	Interviewer	QUICK TEST OF CALIFORNIA – Concord CA

40

KARIN JACOBSON

3230 - 27th Street
San Francisco CA 94114
(415) 556-1888

Objective: Entry level position with film or video production company

SUMMARY OF QUALIFICATIONS

- Production assistant to Associate Producer, Mill Valley Film Festival.
- Special skills in language, creative & journalistic writing, and photography.
- Experience in radio production at university radio station, involving interviewing, taping, reporting, anchoring.
- Degree in Art History, with emphasis in art and graphics.
- Lifelong exposure to film and television industries.

RELATED EXPERIENCE

Film
At Mill Valley Film Festival, as production assistant:
* Developed and coordinated special children's film series.
* Organized & assisted with operational tasks of film institute office: answered phones for staff of 15.
* Planned and implemented operational model for Special Events Dept.

Communication/Media
At KALX Radio, as news writer, anchor and reporter:
* Engineered and anchored a weekly newscast:
  - wrote news stories   - interviewed city officials, students, and faculty
  - taped finished stories   - investigated & reported on student rallies & campus activities.
* Filmed live, on-air radio reports of the Democratic National Convention in July 1984.
* Trained and supervised incoming staff members.

Visual Arts/Design
* Acted in, directed and co-authored independent short 8mm film projects.
* Published photographs in small LA newspaper and university newspaper.
* Designed window displays; earned position as Fashion Coordinator for exclusive boutique in LA.

Promotion/Fundraising/PR
* Obtained donation of office equipment for news department.
* Acquired accounts from local businesses for underwriting and advertising.
* Planned, organized and promoted an all-day music seminar for KALX: contacted (by phone & mail) musicians, agents, managers and laywers; the project grossed over $28,000.

WORK HISTORY

Fall 1985	Production Assistant	MILL VALLEY FILM FESTIVAL
1984-present	Producer	KALX Radio, UC Berkeley
Jan-June '85	Tutor, algebra	WILLARD JR. HIGH SCHOOL - Berkeley
1981-1985	Fulltime student	UC Berkeley & Univ. of Oregon
June '80-Sept '81	Asst. Manager	PAPPA GALLO Shoes - Brentwood CA
Jan- Aug, '79	Fashion Coordinator	JONA Clothing Boutique - Pacific Palisades CA

EDUCATION

B.A., Art History - University of California, Berkeley 1985
Universita di Firenze - Florence, Italy 1983

CHARMAINE BROWN
361 - 25th Ave.
San Francisco CA 94121
339-4421

Objective: Management position in a non-profit organization.

HIGHLIGHTS OF QUALIFICATIONS
- Six years successful supervisory and management experience.
- Resourceful and self-confident; get the job done, and do it well.
- Strong interpersonal and communication skills.
- Extensive experience in design & implementation of training programs.
- Remain calm and work well under demanding conditions.

PROFESSIONAL EXPERIENCE

Management
* Established training programs:
  - Wrote and published yearly training calendars;
  - Located and scheduled instructors for weekly classes in military skills;
  - Coordinated training for personnel dispersed over 1.7 million miles;
  - Forecasted and managed annual training budget while maximizing formal schooling.
* Planned, coordinated and conducted management conferences attended by officers from all over the country.
* Managed a small convenience store, overseeing orders and deliveries, and supervising 3 employees.

Supervision
* Exercised total supervisory responsibility for a unit of 22 technical security personnel:
  - Organized the unit into teams and designated the first-line supervisors;
  - Established an evaluation program, utilizing quarterly written reports;
  - Directed field operations, including planning, budgeting, travel and housing arrangements.
* Successfully planned, organized and led field training missions in a "real-world" environment, ensuring adequate provisions and operational equipment, and providing direction and supervision for 30-40 trainees for up to three weeks.

Written & Oral Communication
* Made presentations and briefings to officials to get approval and funding for operations.
* Wrote and presented information briefings to peer officers to maximize utilization of resources.
* Effectively counseled team leaders and supervisors.
* Authored award recommendations for subordinates that consistently won appproval.
* Compiled and edited comprehensive activity reports from subordinate units for national publication.

WORK HISTORY

1985	Administrative Asst.	ALUMNAE RESOURCES Career Center - SF
1978-84	Chief, Technical Security Branch	US ARMY - San Francisco
"	Battalion Plans & Training Officer	"
"	Chief, Collection Management Section	US ARMY - Germany
"	Platoon Leader	"
1976-78	Student	
1974-75	Manager	BORLAND CORPORATION - Atlanta GA
1973-74	Admin.Asst/Bookkeeper	ATLANTA BANK & TRUST - Atlanta GA

EDUCATION
B.A., German - Georgia State University, Atlanta GA

42

MARK KILLORIN

1219 Parker Street
Albany CA 94706
(415) 425-0632

Objective: Trainee in Real Estate Property Management

HIGHLIGHTS OF QUALIFICATIONS

- Experienced landlord and apartment complex manager
- Licensed in Real Estate Sales
- Certificate in Real Estate from Diablo Valley CC
- Lifelong exposure to family real estate business.
- 10 years experience in retail sales.

RELATED EXPERIENCE

MANAGEMENT

* Managed 18-unit apartment complex:
  - loan collections
  - yard work, maintenance
  - monitor parking
  - tenant complaints/requests
  - screen & research potential tenants
  - install appliances
* Managed warehouse:
  Verified accurate delivery; enforced strict receiving rules; prepared work assignments for night crews; designed & maintained a workable schematic for warehouse stock.
* Assistant Manager sub
  - supervised 35 clerks
  - prepared complex merchandise orders
  - entered transactions on computer
  - performed detailed bookkeeping
  - resolved customer & employee disputes

REAL ESTATE

* Researched and purchased two income properties (a single-family dwelling and a duplex), both generating profit.
* Developed expertise in all aspects of real estate financing.
* Assisted in accounting: loan recording and loan collections.
* Performed market analyses and square-foot analyses for property appraisals.

SALES

* Completed comprehensive course in Real Estate Sales at Diablo Valley College.
* Sold retail products and developed excellent customer rapport for 10 years.
* Participated regularly in team competition for creative marketing displays in a retail store.
* Studied sales reports and reorganized retail stock displays to maximize sales volume.

EMPLOYMENT HISTORY

1975-1985	Warehouse Manager	PARK & SHOP MARKET, Oakland
1983 summer	Asst. Manager	PARK & SHOP MARKET, Oakland
1977-1978	Office Assistant, part time	E.J., KILLORIN Co., Real Estate Loans, Berkeley

EDUCATION & TRAINING

A.A. degree, Business Administration - Diablo Valley College, Pleasant Hill
Real Estate Certificate Program, DVCC | Real Estate Licensing Program, Anthony Schools, Oakland

43

DORIAN UHLER
1315 Martinez Lane
San Leandro CA 94579
(415) 357-0644

Objective: Position as Receptionist/Office Assistant in Chiropractic Office

Highlights of Qualifications
* 8 years experience in office settings; familiar with office procedures.
* Sincere dedication to promoting the healing process.
* Serious professional interest in chiropractic studies.
* Reliable, responsible and efficient.

RELEVANT EXPERIENCE

Office Skills

* Typed forms, letters, reports in a wide variety of office settings.
* Created and maintained filing system for corporate office and court system.
* Developed systematic method for accurately keeping track of customer records.
* Responded to changing priorities, and followed through on instructions, as research assistant to faculty member.

Client Screening & Client Relations

* Assessed health clients' need for information, offered reassurance where needed, and provided detailed descriptions of services available.
* Matched potential therapy patients (at women's health clinic) with appropriate professionals after careful assessment of their needs and the therapists' qualifications.
* Effectively handled customer complaints in a hectic business office by being sensitive to the clients' immediate needs and efficiently clearing up the problem whenever possible.

JOB HISTORY

1983–1985	Fulltime pre-chiropractic student	Merritt College – Oakland
1983–1984	Utility Construction Worker	East Bay Municipal Utilities District – Oakland
" "	Research Assistant	Dr. C. Arrington, history professor
1976–1982	Union Carpenter	Assigned to numerous construction projects
1978–1982	Consultant on Apprenticeship	(by invitation of local colleges and high-schools)
1977–1978	Intake Counselor	Berkeley Women's Center/Mental Health Unit
1974–1976	Customer Relations Rep.	Boise Cascade Office Supplies – Seattle
1973	Inventory Clerk	Genuine Auto Parts Co. – Seattle
1970–1972	Receptionist	King County Juvenile Court – Seattle
1971	Secretary	City Police Dept. – Seattle

EDUCATION

Merritt College – Pre-Chiropractic studies – 1983-85
Griffin Murphy Business College, Seattle – 1972
Seattle Central Community College – 1971-72

44

MARGO SEGALL, R.N.
2131 Blackhawk Road
Lafayette, CA 94549
(415) 275-2347

Objective: Medical investigator/counselor position with Irwin Memorial Blood Bank

HIGHLIGHTS OF QUALIFICATIONS

- Skill in dealing with sensitive populations in a professional and concerned manner.
- Able to work independently and as a cooperative team member.
- Experienced and competent phlebotomist.
- Thorough understanding of the protocols of human research and data collection, through 11 years experience as research clinical nurse.

PROFESSIONAL EXPERIENCE

Counseling
* Conducted crisis intervention and long-term counseling with individuals of diverse backgrounds, dealing with issues of confinement, illness, and institutional group living.
* Advised prospective research volunteers of positive test-results indicating presence of venereal disease, TB, high blood pressure or abnormal blood values.
* Directed disqualified volunteers to appropriate referral agencies as necessary for medical follow-up.

Phlebotomy
* Drew blood samples for high-volume health screenings in over 40 human nutrition research studies.
* Performed venipunctures and/or IVs throughout each study, as specified by research protocol.
* Prepared blood samples for analysis or transport.

Management/Supervision
* Served as head nurse over 6-month period, supervising support staff, research volunteers and graduate students, for a UC Berkeley nutrition-related study.
* Authored procedure on blood/body fluid precautions, and delivered in-service training talk to staff.
* Taught data-collection techniques to research participants.
* Assembled final report data at conclusion of studies.

Knowledge of AIDS
* Familiar with "Guidelines for HTLV-III Antibody Testing in the Community - June, 1985", as provided by the State of California.
* Completed 3 continuing education workshops on AIDS :
  - 10/85 "AIDS: Fears, Facts, and Fantasies" - Letterman Hospital and Shanti Project.
  - 9/84 "AIDS: The Spectrum of the Acquired Immune Deficiency Syndrome" - Letterman Hospital
  - 8/83 "AIDS: Infection Control for Health Workers" - San Francisco Dept. of Public Health

EMPLOYMENT HISTORY

1974-present	Research/Clinical Nurse II	UNIV. OF CALIFORNIA /U.S.D.A. - Berkeley/San Francisco
1981-84	Health Consultant	BERKELEY UNIFIED SCHOOL DIST. (concurrent with above)
1966-70	Teacher, Special Education	RICHMOND UNIFIED SCHOOL DIST.

EDUCATION
B.A., English & Art - UC BERKELEY, 1964 ● Teaching Credential, 1965
R.N. - MERRITT COLLEGE, 1971; **CPR** Certified - 1985

SHERRIE MALLET
5602 Clayton Street – Apt. 34
San Francisco CA 94104
(415) 929-2640

Objective: Position in sales / marketing

SUMMARY OF QUALIFICATIONS
- Honest, straight-forward, respected and trusted by clients who keep coming back.
- Equally effective working in self-managed projects and as member of a team.
- Results oriented professional who doesn't take No for an answer.
- Outstanding communication, analytical and presentation skills.
- Sharp, innovative, quick learner; proven ability to adapt quickly to a challenge.

PROFESSIONAL EXPERIENCE

Marketing, Sales Presentation
* Planned successful strategies to target and develop new accounts.
* Consistently expanded customer base by at least 50%, and increased revenues from current clients by 25%.
* Made oral presentations to upper management of major corporations, such as Bechtel, Union Carbide, Chevron, Lockheed.

Planning/Organizing
* Assessed and evaluated market conditions to identify sources for potential new client base.
* Developed and revised daily, weekly and monthly plans of sales strategies.
* Organized Northern California sales territory to maximize efficiency of calling pattern.

Communications
* Wrote evaluations, problem analyses, and daily plans.
* Wrote timely reports and forecasts to management, on past and projected sales volume.
* Composed product information letters and quotations for clients.
* Restored and maintained good working relations with clients:
  - maintained daily telephone contact with current accounts;
  - made field visits and discussed customers' problems;
  - researched problem areas and provided detailed information;
  - followed through quickly and thoroughly with satisfactory resolutions.

EMPLOYMENT HISTORY

1983–85	District Sales Manager	R.J. COOPER TRUCKING CO. – Emeryville CA
1981–83	Accounts Executive	T.F. AIR FREIGHT CO. – South San Francisco CA
1975–81	Accounts Executive	EAST TEXAS MOTOR FREIGHT – South San Francisco CA
1973–75	Sales Representative	AMERICAN INDUSTRIES INC – San Francisco CA
1968–73	Head Teacher	JEWISH COMMUNITY CENTER – St. Louis MO

EDUCATION
B.S., Education – Ohio State University
Sales/Marketing courses at UC Berkeley,
City College, SF and San Francisco State

MICHELLE OLSON
Consultant in Career Development and Creative Problem Solving

322 Beverly Place - Piedmont, CA 94611
Home: 302-5867   Business: 685-1990

HIGHLIGHTS OF QUALIFICATIONS

- Masters candidate in Career Counseling and Development.
- Outstanding teacher, specializing in conflict resolution and human relations.
- Extensive background in counseling, instructing and program development.
- Highly creative and intuitive problem solver.
- Special talent for drawing people out, and clarifying their problems and needs.

PROFESSIONAL EXPERIENCE

CONSULTANT   **Michelle Olson & Associates - Oakland CA**   **1980 to present**

Consulting: Counseling
- Designed and presented seminars on conflict resolution for business and government agencies, which resulted in increasing the number of employees utilizing EAP counseling services.
- Counseled and motivated individuals to recognize and understand personal needs, problems, alternatives and goals, using a combination of practical problem-solving skills and techniques. My practice has quadrupled in four years.

Instructing
- Developed and implemented courses and workshops for Piedmont Adult Education classes:
  - Effective Listening   - Managing Anger   - Making Good Decisions
  These classes generated additional clients for my private practice, and increased participation in the Adult Education School.
- Contracted to co-teach and develop a "Creativity in Business" course for the MBA program at California State University, Hayward.

Facilitating
- Co-facilitated and collaborated on "Creativity in Business" seminars for Stanford School of Business Alumni Association (Hawaii) and for Young Presidents' Organization (Portland)
- Created and led on-going "Getting Clear" group for women, focused on improving their interpersonal relationship skills.

OWNER/DIRECTOR Aerobic-Exercise Studio - Oakland, CA   **1979-83**

Business Management
- Founded, developed and managed Oakland's first aerobic exercise studio.
- Trained and supervised 8 aerobic instructors, serving more than 300 clients.

Program Development
- Designed and presented workshops on stress management.
  The workshops evolved into a private practice, Michelle Olson & Associates.

EDUCATION

M.A. Candidate, Career Counseling & Development - John F. Kennedy University, Orinda CA
B.A. - Marymount College, Tarrytown, NY
Secondary Teaching Credential, University of California, Berkeley

SUSAN HUTCHEON
2130 Lincoln Ave #5
Berkeley CA 94707
(415) 527-4440

Objective : Position in software support for a computer or software retailer

HIGHLIGHTS OF QUALIFICATIONS

- Exceptional ability to quickly master new software and apply its full range of capabilities.
- Accurately interpret customers' problems and offer the best resolution.
- Outstanding telephone communications; patient, personable and receptive.
- Four years experience with personal computers.

RELEVANT EXPERIENCE

Training
* Trained 7 magazine publishers in computer application to their industry:
  - introduced them to elementary computer use.
  - taught them how to use Remote Copy Input program, designed by my company.
  - advised on which parts of the program applied to their current needs.
  - assisted them on an on-going basis to use increasingly more components of the program.

Troubleshooting / Problem Solving
* Advised clients on what is technically possible or impossible and how to achieve particular printing effects.
* Successfully resolved timing problems between client, production and printer.
* Saved important photo-history data for a client by effectively backtracking to the source of the problem and correcting the original file.
* Reorganized user-areas on customer's hard disk, restoring compatibility of file locations so they were retrievable by the program.

Software Development & Program Application
* Assisted programmers in design of a program to translate computer generated ads into full-page compositions by advising on how typesetting works.
* Identified specific applications for a new program as the package grew.
* Tested newly written programs for any bugs and documented them for the programmer.
* Reported to programmers customer feedback on program weaknesses and strengths.

WORK HISTORY

1980-85	Production Manager	SYSTEMS UNLIMITED CO, Danville CA
1979-80	Assist. to Director of Production	HOMES & LAND PUBLISHING CO, Tallahassee FL
1977-79	Mail Clerk	STATE OF FLORIDA, Tallahassee FL

Some Skills & Skill Areas

(both **transferable** skills and **special-knowledge** skill areas)

Account Management
Accounting
Administration
Advertising
Advocacy
Analysis & Evaluation
Audio-Visual Presentation
Bookkeeping
Budgeting
Business Communications
Business Management
Career Development
Classroom Teaching
Client Services
Communications
Community Organizing
Community Relations
Computer Programming
Computer Usage
Contracts & Agreements
Coordination
Corporate Administration
Cost Analysis
Counseling
Curriculum Development
Customer Relations
Customer Service
Data Processing
Decorating
Display
Drafting
Editing

Electronics Engineering
Employee Relations
Environmental Planning
Equipment Maintenance
Expense Reduction
Family Counseling
Field Research
Film & Video
Financial Planning
Food Preparation
Forecasting
Fundraising
Graphic Design & Layout
Group Benefits
Inspection & Maintenance
Interviewing
Inventory Control
Investigation/Research
Labor Relations
Language Interpreting
Management Analysis
Market Research
Marketing
Media
Mediation
Merchandising
Negotiation
Office Management
Outreach
Performing Arts
Personnel Training
Photography

Policy Making
Presentation
Printing
Product Development
Production
Program Design
Promotion and Publicity
Public Relations
Public Speaking
Publishing
Purchasing
Quality Control
Real Estate
Records Management
Recruiting
Reporting
Resource Development
Restaurant Management
Retailing
Sales (Inside; Outside)
Special Education
Statistical Analysis
Supervision
Systems Analysis
Teaching
Technical Writing
Telecommunications
Testing
Training
Visual Arts
Word Processing
Writing

Action Verbs

Adapted, enlarged list inspired by Employment Development Department of Palo Alto, CA.

Management Skills

administered
analyzed
assigned
attained
chaired
contracted
consolidated
coordinated
delegated
developed
directed
evaluated
executed
improved
increased
organized
oversaw
planned
prioritized
produced
recommended
reviewed
scheduled
strengthened
supervised

Communication Skills

addressed
arbitrated
arranged
authored
corresponded
developed
directed
drafted
edited
enlisted
formulated
influenced
interpreted
lectured
mediated
moderated
motivated
negotiated
persuaded
promoted
publicized
reconciled
recruited
spoke
translated
wrote

Research Skills

clarified
collected
critiqued
diagnosed
evaluated
examined
extracted
identified
inspected
interpreted
interviewed
investigated
organized
reviewed
summarized
surveyed
systematized

Technical Skills

assembled
built
calculated
computed
designed
devised
engineered
fabricated
maintained
operated
overhauled
programmed
remodeled
repaired
solved
trained
upgraded

Teaching Skills

adapted
advised
clarified
coached
communicated
coordinated
developed
enabled
encouraged
evaluated
explained
facilitated
guided
informed
initiated
instructed
persuaded
set goals
stimulated

Financial Skills

administered
allocated
analyzed
appraised
audited
balanced
budgeted
calculated
computed
developed
forecast
managed
marketed

planned
projected
researched

Creative Skills

acted
conceptualized
created
designed
developed
directed
established
fashioned
founded
illustrated
instituted
integrated
introduced
invented
originated
performed
planned
revitalized
shaped

Helping Skills

assessed
assisted
clarified
coached
counseled
demonstrated
diagnosed
educated
expedited
facilitated
familiarized
guided
referred
rehabilitated
represented

Clerical or Detail Skills

approved
arranged
catalogued
classified
collected
compiled
dispatched
executed
generated
implemented
inspected
monitored
operated
organized
prepared
processed
purchased
recorded
retrieved
screened
specified
systematized
tabulated
validated

Cover Letters

Cover letters are EXTREMELY important.

Here's what a Damn Good Cover Letter needs to do:

1) **Address someone in authority** (by name and title) who could hire you. When IMPOSSIBLE to get that information, use their functional title ("Dear Manager,") even if you have to guess ("Dear Selection Committee").

2) **Demonstrate that you've done some "homework"** on the company and can see THEIR point of view (their current problems, their interests and priorities).

3) **Convey your enthusiasm and commitment**—or even passion—for this line of work.

4) **Balance professionalism with personal warmth and friendliness.** Avoid like the plague using generic, say-nothing, alienating phrases like "enclosed please find," "Dear Sir or Madam"! This is a PERSONAL letter.

5) **Identify at least one thing about you that's unique**—say, a special gift for getting along with all kinds of people—something that goes beyond the basic requirements of the position, that distinguishes you, AND is relevant to the position. (Then, if several others are equally qualified, there's a reason to pick YOU.)

6) **Be appropriate** to the field you're exploring—STAND OUT, but in a non-gimmicky way.

7) **Outline specifically what you are asking** and offering.

8) **Point directly to the next step,** telling just what YOU intend to do next.

9) **Remain as brief and focused as possible.**

This is NOT EASY to do! A Damn Good Cover Letter is truly a work of art.

Following are some examples.

Sample Cover Letters

NOTE: all sample cover letters in this book, like the sample resumes, are from "real life," developed by, for and with the author's clients. Nothing is "made up," but details are changed to protect people's privacy.

This cover letter accompanies a resume sent after a brief phone conversation with an employer about an advertised opening. The employer asked for a resume and references.

January 18, 1985
784 Capital Street #3
Oakland, CA 94610

Mr. Donald Schmidt
Equitec Financial Group
8055 Portland Street
San Rafael, CA 94901

Dear Mr. Schmidt:

Enclosed is my resume with three references which you requested during our telephone conversation last Friday.

I was pleased to learn that Equitec Financial Group had an opening for the position of Mortgage Acquisitions Analyst. Besides the favorable comment in the Wall Street Journal, I've also read good commentaries on your company in other publications. I value professionalism and thoroughness in myself and in others. From what I know so far about Equitec, it's a respected professional group.

You pointed out that you are effectively filling four positions with two people. I appreciate the level of commitment you referred to and in fact am looking for a career that allows me to dissolve the boundaries that often exist between a person's job and the rest of his life.

I believe I'm capable of mastering the concepts we discussed relating to present value and the use of calculators. I subscribe to a financial newsletter, *The Creative Financing Report*, and I think I have the aptitude and temperament for that aspect of the job. I also enjoy sales; my resume shows my orientation in that regard.

Based on our conversation I believe I would be able to contribute to Equitec Financial Group. I have enclosed a copy of my resume, and look forward to hearing from you soon.

Sincerely,

Frank Winne

This cover letter accompanied a resume sent after Mark did some local exploration and followed up on a lead from a family friend; he hopes to uncover an entry level position in this new field. The objective on Mark's resume (see page 43) reads "Trainee Position in Real Estate Property Management."

June 14, 1985
1219 Parker Street
Albany, CA 94706
Tel. 425-0632

Arthur Goodwin, Manager
Coldwell Banker Real Estate
1495 Shattuck Ave.
Berkeley, CA 94709

Dear Mr. Goodwin,

Recently I've been researching the local real estate market to identify a company that is respected in the field and offers a good sales training program, and the name of Coldwell Banker came up repeatedly as "the number one company."

I have had a lifelong interest in real estate, having been exposed to it since childhood through the family business (started by my grandfather) which provides funds for financing real estate.

Recently on my own I purchased two income properties; I enjoyed this work, and have been successful in identifying profit-generating properties. As you'll see on my attached resume, I have also taken classes in real estate, received a certificate, and have my salesman's license.

With my background, enthusiasm and training, I think I would have much to contribute to Coldwell Banker's sales program and I'd like to come in and talk with you about it in person.

I will call your office on Thursday, June 20 to see if a convenient meeting time can be arranged.

Sincerely,

Mark Killorin

Amy responds to an ad for newspaper "interns" (unpaid trainees), which fits her situation.

951 Clement St.
San Francisco, CA 94118
Tel. 211-9898
October 6, 1984

Bay Guardian
2700 19th St.
San Francisco, CA 94110

Dear Staff,

I am very interested in your advertisement for interns. An internship with the BAY GUARDIAN is an ideal opportunity for me to sharpen my research and writing skills at a paper I enjoy and for which I am eager to work. My level of skill is ideal to assist you in producing current, accurate information for news stories; at the same time I would benefit greatly from the experience and expertise of your staff.

As a regular reader of the GUARDIAN, I've come to rely on your investigative reporting of pertinent political issues and local candidates, and I would like very much to be part of your team. I will be pleased to meet with you at your convenience.

Sincerely,

Amy K. Lifchette

This cover letter responds to a newspaper ad, "SALES, cookie & cracker. Nationally famous cookie, cracker & snack co. has exc. career opportunities for aggressive people in the peninsula area...." Notice that Donna refers to her career search, including the use of "info interviewing."

1224 Seymour Ave.
Walnut Creek, CA 94598
August 26, 1985

Manager, Sales Department
P.O. Box 64375
Hayward, CA 94545

Dear Manager,

This is in response to your ad in Sunday's Examiner/Chronicle, seeking a salesperson. I was excited when I read your ad since I've had a long-time interest in food sales, and your product line sounds particularly appealing to me. In the course of my recent career research, I spent some time interviewing and accompanying a sales rep for a well known cookie and snack food manufacturer; from that experience I discovered that I have the personality, aggressiveness and persuasive manner required in this line of work.

I would be delighted to talk with you in person about this position, and look forward to hearing from you soon. I may be reached at 399-1667, where my answering machine can take your message if I'm out.

Sincerely,

Donna Katzen

Another letter in response to an ad in the same paper:

August 21, 1985

Selection Committee
1293 Ninth Avenue
San Francisco, CA 94117

Dear Committee,

In response to your recent ad for a freelance Spanish-speaking editor/copyeditor, appearing in the San Francisco CHRONICLE, I am submitting a resume outlining my qualifications for the job. I believe I have excellent credentials for this work, and would like the opportunity to work again with educational materials using my native language.

I am currently teaching several classes at City Community College, and this freelance assignment would fit my schedule very well. I would be pleased to come in and discuss this further with you.

You may contact me by leaving a message at my work place, Valley Language Vocational School, telephone 488-8324. The best time to reach me in person is between noon and 2 pm at that number, or at home before 10 am, 526-0880.

I am looking forward to hearing from you soon.

Sincerely,

Miriam P. Cuthbertson

54

Margaret's resume is found in this book on page 24. Here is her accompanying cover letter:

333 Cityview Highway
Oakland, CA 94606
655-9941

Ms. Molly Radley
Management Employment
Pacific Telephone
44 Montgomery Street
San Francisco, CA 94101

Dear Ms. Radley,

I was excited to learn of your "College Hire Program," in particular that position titled "Systems Assistant." It is the first training program I have encountered that seemed perfectly suited to me.

For the past 15 years as a teacher, I have taught all grade levels and virtually all subjects. This flexibility and adaptability has been an asset to the school district and provided me with an openness to change and a confidence in new settings.

My fascination with computers is not new; two years ago I participated in an in-service computer programming class using the BASIC language, and have currently been volunteering with an organization where I have received training as a computer operator. In addition I am enrolled in a data processing class at the College of Marin.

I would like to work with Pacific Telephone as a Systems Assistant and have enclosed my resume. I would also be open to discussing other positions in which you feel I could benefit Pacific Telephone. I'll call your office in a week, and hope we can then make an appointment to discuss this.

Sincerely,

Margaret Roberts

Richard is answering an ad in COMPUTERWORLD magazine.

March 31, 1985
1421 Sacramento St.
El Cerrito, CA 94530
(415) 263-4441

Ms. Lydia Tranier
The Green Valley Group, Inc.
P.O. Box 11114
Green Valley, CA 95843

Dear Ms. Tranier,

I was attracted to your notice of a systems programmer position with The Green Valley Group, which appeared in "Computerworld" March 21. As my attached resume will show, I have a fairly extensive and diverse background in data processing and I believe that I have a great deal to offer to your organization. I have used both mainframe and micro based systems on a range of applications in both large and small organizations, and have always enjoyed a position with challenge.

Your brief position announcement mentioned a DEC VAX machine, and I am interested to know the types of applications you support. I would enjoy the opportunity to visit Green Valley and would like to meet with you to discuss how well my skills might fit your needs for a data processing professional, and also to learn more about your organization.

Sincerely,

Richard Fodor

*Margo's letter does everything a good cover letter should do (see page 51), including a reference to what **she** plans to do next—taking the initiative, without being "pushy." Margo's resume appears on page 45.*

1722 Blackhawk Road
Lafayette, CA 94549
(415) 275-2347
December 12, 1985

Katherine Sullivan
Irwin Memorial Blood Bank
270 Masonic Avenue
San Francisco, CA 94118

Dear Ms. Sullivan,

As you suggested in our recent brief phone conversation, I am sending a resume which outlines my qualifications and professional expertise related to the position of Medical Investigator at Irwin Memorial Blood Bank.

When I learned of this possible opening through my friend, Diane Levenson, I became immediately intrigued because the job appears to relate so directly to my past experience as a research nurse and to my current interest and concern over the AIDS crisis.

I would find it very gratifying to contribute my professional skills to AIDS related research. I also believe I would be effective as well as empathetic in working with the people who learn that they test positive for the HTLV-III antibody.

Early next week I will call your office in hopes that we can arrange an appointment to talk in person about this position. If it's more convenient for you, I can be reached in the evening at my home phone number, listed above.

Sincerely,

Margo Segall

*Another kind of cover letter, a **"broadcast letter,"** is a letter sent to several different companies at once, when there is **not** a known job opening and you are asking for an exploratory interview anyway. If your Broadcast Letter has enough detail (such as the one below) you could send it INSTEAD of a resume. Otherwise, it might ACCOMPANY your resume.*

900 McGregor St.
Berkeley, CA 94708
835-3399
April 28, 1985

Mr. Cortland Richardson
Program Sales Manager
Xerox Corporation
1 California St.
San Francisco, CA 94111

Dear Mr. Richardson:

Your firm came to my attention while I was doing career research to locate companies that have a quality product and offer in-service training in my desired area, which is sales/marketing and management.

I would like an opportunity to talk with you in person about your personnel needs and to present some of my experience and accomplishments which I believe may relate to them.

In eight years of extensive professional contact, these are some highlights of my experience:

- I wrote a successful grant proposal which brought my organization $25,000, enabling us to create an additional fulltime position.
- I designed, implemented and promoted an innovative arts therapy project, for which I succeeded in attracting volunteer guest artists and contributions of free supplies, and greatly increased client participation.
- I supervised two staff persons as coordinator of a new follow-up services system which I developed, resulting in expanded and higher-quality outreach to clients resistant to agency visits.

It would be my pleasure to discuss further details of my business experience as related to your firm's future staff requirements. I'll be calling your office in a few days to see if an appointment can be arranged. (I can be reached at 415-540-6888 if you should prefer to call me before then.)

Yours truly,

Lee Anne Wilcox

Ten Tough Questions

About Resumes

1. "How do I account for that year when I wasn't employed?"
2. "What if I was 'just a housewife' for 20 years?"
3. "What do I do about dates on my job history . . . when I had two or three little jobs with a month or so in between?"
4. "What if I was called a 'secretary' and never got the pay or job title for all the things I really did?"
5. "Can't I skip the Job Objective? I don't want to limit myself."
6. "What if I don't have any work experience in the exact job that I want now?"
7. "How long should a resume be? One page?"
8. "What if my experience was from a long time ago?"
9. "What if they insist on a chronological resume and a lot of dates?"
   and finally . . .
10. "How should I use my resume?"

---

1. "HOW DO I ACCOUNT FOR THAT YEAR WHEN I WASN'T EMPLOYED?"

Tell the truth, creatively.

BE POSITIVE; refer to what you WERE doing rather than to what you WEREN'T doing. Don't say "unemployed" because it MIGHT convey an UN-truth about you, that you aren't interested in working, when in fact we both know you WANT to work. Instead, look at what you WERE doing, allow yourself a reasonable degree of "being human," and emphasize the positive aspects of what you did that year.

EXAMPLE: Candidly from my own experience . . . in 1974 I was traveling across the country "trying to figure out what to do with the rest of my life," coping with an unexpected traumatic illness, making some embarrassing and painful and wonderful experiments in group-living, and looking — sometimes desperately — for work that I could feel good about. I got by on unemployment for awhile, Medi-Cal for the illness, off-and-on Kelly Girl work, and loans from Mom. It was a very tough year.

What does it say on my resume?

"1974 — Travel and independent study"

And that's true! I've just expressed it with more dignity than I was feeling at the time. I don't need to tell anybody, on my resume, what a bummer that year was. And believe me, I learned enough to justify calling it "independent study"!

---

2. "WHAT IF I WAS 'JUST A HOUSEWIFE' FOR 20 YEARS?"

Change your attitude, for starters (more below);
Give yourself credit for all you've accomplished and learned;
Then, get help expressing it all creatively.

Every woman I've worked with, who started with "just a housewife" self-image, ended up with greatly improved self-esteem after doing a DAMN GOOD RESUME. When you discard the myth that only PAID work is valuable, and start listing everything you ever did (home management activities, volunteer work, hobby and craft work, personal growth projects, reading of all kinds), an impressive body of skills, knowledges and experience emerges.

The task then is simply to identify what skills are demonstrated in all that, and learning to express them in world-of-work terms. Get help and support from places like "Displaced Homemaker" centers and community Women's Centers for the needed attitude change, and help in analyzing and writing about your skills. (Refer also to Deana's resume in Appendix A.)

---

3. "WHAT DO I DO ABOUT DATES ON MY JOB HISTORY? . . . WHEN I HAD TWO OR THREE LITTLE JOBS, WITH A MONTH OR SO IN BETWEEN?"

Delete very short-term jobs, OR
Combine several short jobs in one description. (See Deana's resume.)
Stick to YEARS rather than precise dates by-the-month. Rounding off to years is a good general practice anyway:
   — it looks better
   — it keeps the reader from doing a lot of detailed arithmetic with your work record when you want them to focus on your SKILLS. Read the Employer Feedback section; employers have different opinions on this.

4. "WHAT IF I WAS CALLED A 'SECRETARY' AND NEVER GOT THE PAY OR THE JOB TITLE FOR ALL THE THINGS I REALLY DID?"

You don't have to use THEIR job title! So MUCH fine and important work is done every day in millions of offices by intelligent women who aren't being adequately paid or recognized for the high levels of their skills and responsibilities.

"COME THE REVOLUTION . . . " Meanwhile, feel free to create a fairer job title that reflects the highest level of skills you used as a so-called "secretary."

EXAMPLE: One client's old resume listed "secretary" positions five times. Her NEW DAMN GOOD RESUME refers to those same jobs with the following reasonable, fair job titles:

    office supervisor
    director's assistant
    technical writer
    executive secretary
    administrative assistant

DIRECTOR OF OFFICE OPERATIONS

5. "CAN'T I JUST SKIP THE JOB OBJECTIVE? I DON'T WANT TO LIMIT MYSELF."

NO!

Clearly stating your Objective serves to FOCUS you, not to box you in. It's critically important to KNOW WHAT YOUR OBJECTIVE IS, as explicitly as possible, and to state it, and then to have everything else on your resume directly relate to it. THAT'S what makes it a DAMN GOOD RESUME.

And remember, you could have TWO or more resumes, each with different objectives. Look at George's two resumes in the Sample Resume section for examples.

6. "WHAT IF I DON'T HAVE ANY WORK EXPERIENCE IN THE EXACT JOB THAT I WANT TO DO NOW?"

A DAMN GOOD RESUME is the perfect format for you. If you really want a particular kind of job and are confident that you'd do well at it if only you got the chance, it's just about certain that you have enough transferable skills to show that you're a good candidate for the job.

Here's what your resume needs to show:

Transferable skills from paid or unpaid experience.

A credible progression from where you've been to where you want to go now. (If there's a leap the size of the Grand Canyon from where you are to the position you want, then be willing to state a current objective that bridges the gap.)

Evidence of motivation & potential—experience that used the same kind of personality traits and strengths that your Ideal Job calls for. (See Shari's resume on page 27.)

7. "HOW LONG SHOULD A RESUME BE?"

One page is best, occasionally two. And it WILL all fit—even if you have 25 years of fantastic experience. A good resume is like a handful of Aces . . . you DON'T deal out the whole deck! Prospective employers don't WANT your whole life history; they only need to see the essential points that make you qualified, plus the unique experience and attitudes that make you SPECIAL. Say the minimum, powerfully.

8. "WHAT IF MY EXPERIENCE WAS FROM A LONG TIME AGO?"

The employer's attention is turned to your SKILLS, which appear first, rather than WHEN you acquired them, with THE DAMN GOOD RESUME format. Also, you can include your more recent activities of all kinds and show how the skills you acquired are transferable to the job you now seek.

9. "WHAT IF THEY INSIST ON A CHRONOLOGICAL RESUME, WITH ALL THOSE DATES IN ORDER?"

You could point out that your resume DOES include a list of your jobs and the years you did them; it's at the end, and it's condensed. OR, you may decide to go for the chronological resume instead of the D.G.R. format. Some knowledgeable folks insist that a chronological resume is sometimes better — like when you're staying in the same field and trying to move up the career ladder.

This question usually comes up in connection with a Job Application... which you are going to AVOID filling out until after you've had a personal interview with the Hiring Person. THEN attach your resume instead of filling out the "Job History" section, which is invariably designed to your disadvantage. You DO NOT have to give all that information before being interviewed.

EXCEPTION: for civil service jobs, we're advised, your application won't get processed unless you fill it out fully. In that case, don't fight it... do it THEIR way!

10. "HOW SHOULD I USE MY RESUME?"

a) AS A "FIRST DRAFT" MODEL FOR A TAILORED RESUME. Always, when you apply for a specific advertised job opening, rewrite your resume using:
- THEIR job title as your Job Objective (word for word)
- THEIR stated skill requirements as your Skill Areas

b) AS A LAST RESORT FIRST CONTACT. When there's no way around it and you simply can't make the initial contact any other way. (But be creative... there usually is another way to reach the Hiring Person.) Send an excellent cover letter along with your resume.

c) BEFORE YOUR JOB INTERVIEW. To get you focused and clear. Tuck the resume in your pocket to look at just before you enter the new workplace; it will remind you of your objective and of your skills, in case you tend to space out about them.

d) AFTER YOUR JOB INTERVIEW. You can leave it with the employer as a concrete reminder and documentation of the information you provided during the interview. DO NOT hand it to the employer at the beginning of your meeting; she'll be looking at it instead of at you!

e) WHEN YOU MAKE PHONE CALLS TO STRANGERS for job information research. When lining up informational interviews, and such — especially if your morale is flagging — keep your DAMN GOOD RESUME in front of you as you work, to remind you of your skills and accomplishments, and to keep your mind from going blank about your objective.

The Acid Test

What do employers think of THE DAMN GOOD RESUME?

We asked a panel of seven employers to carefully review a sampling of the resumes that appeared in this Guide, and to give us some really "hard-nosed" criticism. Then the resumes in this updated edition were revised to conform to what the employers say they want to see.

In addition, here's a generous sampling of the comments we got from the employers; you'll probably be interested in the field of each of the reviewing employers.

"OB" is Director of a county housing authority.
"RN" is a Vice-President at a large bank.
"CC" is Director of a university placement office.
"HK" is co-owner of a traffic engineering firm.
"JS" is Executive Director of a nonprofit community agency.
"BO" is Co-Director of a privately-funded agency supporting work options.
"LM" is Manager of a systems analysis group at a university.

 Q What about the format of these resumes?

BO: The format is super. I like the sections and their sequence. Nice and clean looking.

OB: Laid out nicely; categories are clear; generally good.

LM: The resumes are really great. I like the approach of tailoring the resume to the objective. The format seems to work for almost everybody. And I like having the material LIMITED to stuff that's related to the work.

CC: I have a difficult time reading each of the clusters of skills; it takes too much time; but also I don't like straight chronological resumes with the dates to the left. I like a resume that accentuates JOB TITLES, tells how long in each job, a few brief lines about major accomplishments. It should be brief, to the point, and relate back to the specific job.

HK: A format like Dee Ann's is easy to scan; the eye focuses on organized material. You should use as few headings as possible. I don't want to study a lot of stuff, I want to GET THE MOST FOR THE LEAST AMOUNT OF TIME, and I want it to look attractive.

HK: Underlining is extremely helpful. It's important to me to be able to FIND what I'm looking for and highlighting it with underlining is real helpful.

Q What about the Job Objective?

OB: I hate getting a resume with a totally unrelated Job Objective; tailor it to the job you're applying for. And don't say "with opportunity for advancement"; instead, name your long-range objective specifically — like a job title — and then add "now looking for experience which allows me to advance to that."

JS: Don't just say "management"; specify management of WHAT.

LM: In the university setting, I haven't seen a resume specifically tailored to the job, though I like that approach.

RN: I don't pay much attention to it because it's usually too general, so I read past it quickly; I'd rather that be handled in the cover letter.

HK: I prefer a simple objective, rather than a long-winded one; I'm turned off by "provides opportunity for advancement" because it seems presumptuous — I want to make that decision.

 Q What do you want in the "One-Liner" statements under the Skill Areas?

OB: I want brief sentences with ACTION words. Refer to RESULTS of your activity; if you were successful, say so. QUANTIFY — what SIZE of a group did you work with, HOW MANY people did you supervise? Don't start sentences with "dealt with" or "responsible for." Select words carefully and be specific. Employers want enough detail to be able to tell a) the level of responsibility, and b) your skills that were involved in it.

JS: I want to know WHERE you got the experience and HOW LONG you did it.

LM: Quantifying, like "improved profits by a million dollars," isn't appropriate in a university setting but it would be if you were in sales or marketing. It matters WHAT the job is whether you use that kind of statement.

RN: I don't like general statements in a resume; it should be a description of ACCOMPLISHED WORK. I want to know what you've done, and where, that makes you qualified for the job. I'm not interested in what people THINK they can do, I want to know what they HAVE DONE.

HK: Speaking and writing skills are very important in our work, because most of what we do is communicating . . . so if you're good at writing reports, SAY SO, even have a special heading for it; even before technical credentials, we look for that. (Note: HK is in the traffic engineering field.)

HK: Using "Restaurant Experience" in Dee Ann's resume is a much better skill heading than "related experience" or "professional experience"; that's good — specific.

Q Is it okay with you that we've extracted the skills-details out from the job titles and presented them under skill-groups instead?

OB: Yes.

LM: Definitely okay with me. I can always look down at the job history to see where they came from.

RN: It took me awhile to figure that out . . . but yes, it's okay with me.

HK: That's excellent. The old way we did our resumes was very difficult to read.

(Not all employers addressed this question, but none expressed objection.)

Q Do you like the qualifications summary, as in Valerie's and Martha's resumes?

OB: Nice; I like the shift of typestyle in Valerie's resume.

BO: I'm distracted by the summary being in a different typeface and being at the bottom. Put it before or after the Employment section.

JS: I like the summary of qualifications at the end of Valerie's resume.

CC: Martha's summary is nice, but repetitious.

HK: The summary in Valerie's is a bonus; I find that useful.

(Obviously, employers aren't in agreement about everything related to resumes.)

Q Please comment on the employment history section.

CC: I want to see JOB TITLES; I'm less interested in the name of the company.

OB: Leave out any job history that's not relevant to the job objective.

JS: I'd prefer more specific information about time, e.g., 3 months, 10 months, 3½ years, etc. I don't like resumes to be TOO general.

LJ: The generalized dates are okay; if I need to check references — which I only do after an interview — I can ask about it then.

(Again, notice the differing opinions.)

Q Any comments on the education section?

CC: The DEGREE is one of the first things I look for; also I look for what is the MAJOR, and usually it's buried somewhere, and that's frustrating.

JS: I want to see the DATE of graduation from college.

OB: Leave out high school reference when you have college. Begin with the bachelor degree.

HK: For engineering, we need to see what KIND of engineering; they could say "specializing in the following . . ." Also, we need to see their credentials; are they a registered engineer? What are their affiliations (organizations).

Q How do you feel about self-appraisal statements?

(NOTE: Employers are responding here to Dee Ann's resume which originally included the statement "energetic, outgoing, honest, reliable, and take pride in my work," which was deleted from the current revision of this GUIDE.)

JS: I like it.

OB: I'm turned off by those statements.

BO: Feels out of place when included with the one-liners; if used, it should be separated out and appear as the last line of Experience.

(Probably best to use self-appraisal statements with caution.)

Q What about references? Should they be mentioned?

OB: Yes, say "references upon request"; I would list some specific people who have some clout in the industry, who are respected and recognized.

LM: I'd like to see "references can be provided." Otherwise it's awkward for the employer to ask, but if it's explicitly stated then I don't mind asking for them.

RN: Yes, but you have to make arrangements about it. For example, I can legally only give out, to a caller, the date a person started work here and when they ended work, and the entry and leaving salary, and the name of the position. That's all. Without specific permission from the ex-employee I can't, by federal law and state law, evaluate their performance or say whether I'd hire them again. I have to have their explicit permission to do that.

Q How many pages is okay for a resume? We hear they should only be one page long.

OB: For management jobs you SHOULD have a two-page resume because an experienced manager should generate two pages of experience.

JS: Two pages is fine.

BO: I'd rather see two pages than have things scrunched onto one page. (HK agrees.)

LM: I don't mind a resume being two pages long, but it should be printed front-and-back so it still goes on one piece of paper.

HK: Two pages is okay with me, but if you go to two pages then use the Summary. Start with the Objective, then right under it the Summary, then the details.

(These responses were a bit of a surprise to the author!)

Q What about cover letters?

MUST HAVE A COVER LETTER — ADDRESSED TO _ME_ !

CC: We require both a resume and a letter of application (cover letter). If people write an excellent letter, then we'd check the resume to see if they meet the basic requirements and call them in for an interview.

OB: They should have brief statements, and include info on how they can be reached.

RN: I'd want to see a personal cover letter addressed to me; that makes a tremendous difference. I don't want it to feel mass-distributed. I place a great deal of importance on the cover letter; in our division, writing is very important. Some of the best applications have been LETTERS ONLY, incorporating at the end a brief summary of experience, and always a reference to a person who can be contacted.

Another reason why A LETTER IS IMPORTANT is that when they write a personalized letter I feel they're showing some interest in working for us, and they've done some homework about this company. It increases my sense of their interest in US, and not that they're just casting out a general net.

 Any other problems you have with people's resumes?

CC: TOO MANY SECTIONS — five or six; I don't want to read all that. I want the info that relates to the job requirements as we sent them out, and I want things to JUMP OUT at me on the resume.

OB: People AREN'T SPECIFIC ENOUGH and they DON'T QUANTIFY. They're TOO GENERAL and then I don't get the answer to my main question, which is, "What makes this person SPECIAL?"

HK: One thing I never want to see on a resume is stuff like hobbies or that they're healthy and have three kids! I don't CARE if they're into swimming, but the schools actually TEACH them to put that stuff on a resume. We laugh when we see that. We're only interested in the quality of the work and the presentation of the person.

 What else is important to you, about resumes?

OB: NO TYPOGRAPHICAL ERRORS whatsoever. Excessive punctuation is distracting, like lots of colons and semicolons. (BO concurs.) PAPER? It's not really important to me, not an issue, though it is to some people.

CC: DON'T MAKE PRINTED RESUMES. I don't like them, especially in the education field. We don't have a lot of money, and I make the assumption that they won't fit in with us if they spent that much on a printed resume. BUT, the resume should LOOK PROFESSIONAL. Use the best quality paper and have the cover letter, resume and envelope all on matching paper. And type the resume specifically for THIS job, with no errors whatever, and don't spend a lot of money.

RN: NO PRINTING. Thank God you aren't advising people to PRINT their resume; that would be CRAZY. A printed resume is far less impressive to me; it has a mass-distribution effect.

 Any more advice for job hunters?

CC: BE READY FOR THE INTERVIEW. Most people are NOT. You need to do a really good deal of research about yourself. Get ready for the interview by:

- knowing what the job is about
- knowing why you're applying
- knowing how you're qualified.

RN: DO SEND A RESUME, even if you don't know of an opening. We get around 12 a week in this division alone; personnel sends them around to the section heads and we review them and say "no" or "yes I'm interested, worth an interview." Often, maybe one gets such a response. If I don't have a job in my department, I can call another department head and ask them to interview the person.

RN: DON'T JUST SHOW UP. I'll NEVER talk to anyone without having a letter in hand first. The RUDEST thing a person can do is to either show up in the reception area without an appointment, or to call up and say "I'm down the street, can I stop in and see you?" I have a busy schedule; I'll be glad to set up an appointment to see a person, but it needs to be at a time that's mutually convenient.

RN: BE PREPARED FOR THE INTERVIEW. Be ready to answer the question, "Why do you want to work for this company?" In our case (large bank) a major question I ask is, "Do you think you'd be comfortable working in a large corporation where things would be fairly structured?" A lot of young people nowadays are turned off by that, but it's important for people to feel at ease at work, so they should ask themselves that question.
RANK YOUR STRONG POINTS. Come in knowing that, and it saves a lot of energy.
KNOW YOUR SALARY EXPECTATIONS. A lot of people will not give me ANY CLUE at all. Don't be bashful or coy about it; I need to know if people's expectations are commensurate with what I can offer. Also, I give a person "extra points" if they ask, "If I take this job, what can I expect to be making five years from now?" Be sure to look into the firm's compensation policy before accepting the job.

Skill Assessment Worksheets

Skill Areas: A. _____

B. _____

C. _____

D. _____

E. _____

F. _____

Skill   "O N E — L I N E R S"

_____ 1. _____

_____

_____ 2. _____

_____

_____ 3. _____

_____

_____ 4. _____

_____

_____ 5. _____

_____

_____ 6. _____

_____

_____ 7. _____

_____

(The space to the left is for entering "A," "B," "C," etc.—whatever
Skill Area(s) is closely related to this One-Liner.)

Skill

_____   8. _____

_____

_____   9. _____

_____

_____   10. _____

_____

_____   11. _____

_____

_____   12. _____

_____

_____   13. _____

_____

_____   14. _____

_____

_____   15. _____

_____

_____   16. _____

_____

_____   17. _____

_____

Skill Area "A": _____
Relevant "One-Liners":
No:

—   _____
    _____

—   _____
    _____

—   _____
    _____

—   _____
    _____

—   _____
    _____

Skill Area "B": _____
Relevant "One-Liners":
No:

—   _____
    _____

—   _____
    _____

—   _____
    _____

—   _____
    _____

—   _____
    _____

Skill Area " ": _____
Relevant "One-Liners":
No:

—— _____

_____

_____

—— _____

_____

_____

—— _____

_____

_____

—— _____

_____

_____

—— _____

_____

Skill Area " ": _____
Relevant "One-Liners":
No:

—— _____

_____

_____

—— _____

_____

_____

—— _____

_____

_____

—— _____

_____

_____

—— _____

_____

How To Use These Worksheets:
An Example

1

Skill Assessment Worksheets

Skill Areas:
A. _Networking_
B. _Researching Resources / Organizing materials_
C. _Teaching_
D. _Writing / Editing_
E. _Counseling / Advising_
F. _____

"ONE – LINERS"

Skill

B 1. _Contacted hundreds of community agencies to update & index counselors' resource manual_

(E) + A 2. _Advised people on how to conduct effective housing search & handle issues, as local resource person for group living_

D 3. _Edited book on Women's Self-led Career Groups_

C 4. _Taught typing and office practice_

(C) E 5. _Taught 6-session, "Field Visits to Bay Area Collective Homes"_

B 6. _Developed greatly improved filing system for extensive engineering design materials_

(C) or D 7. _Developed series of informative hand-outs on local housing sources_

(The space to the left is for entering ... to this One-Liner.)

2

MORE ONE – LINERS

Skill

(D) / C 8. _Co-authored group self-assessment questionnaire in widespread local use_

C 9. _Taught "Massage for Beginners"_

C or (E) 10. _Consulted w/scores of individuals on business writing, teaching them to analyze & present their experience_

(D) or C 11. _Wrote & self published instruction manual, "Better Business Letters"_

(D) A 12. _Initiated & produced 12-24 page Monthly Newsletter for 24 consecutive issues._

(A) B 13. _Assembled materials & reports on cooperative living/working projects around the country_

E/C/(A) 14. _Advised callers on how to make connections + find ... cooperatives + collective groups_

3

Skill Area "A": _Networking_
Relevant "One-Liners":
No:

13 _Assembled materials & reports on cooperative living/working projects around the country_ } _Combine_

14 _Advised callers on how to make connections + find data on coops & communal groups_

Skill Area "B": _Researching Resources / Organizing Materials_
Relevant "One-Liners":
No:

1. _Contacted hundreds of community agencies to update & index counselors' resource manual_

6. _Developed greatly improved filing system for extensive engineering design materials_

Skill Area "C": Teaching   (Combine with "E" –
Relevant "One-Liners":   Counseling / Advising)
No:

4   Taught typing & office practice

5   Taught 6-session " field visits to Bay
    Area Collective Homes "   } Combine

9   Taught "Massage for Beginners".

Skill Area "D": Writing & Editing
Relevant "One-Liners":
No:

3   Edited book on women's self-led career groups

7   Developed series of informative hand-outs   } Combine

8   Co-authored group self-assessment questionnaire
    in widespread local use

11 Wrote + self published instruction manual,
    "Better Business Letters"

12 Initiated + produced 12-24 page monthly
    newsletter for 24 consecuti-

5

Skill Area "E: Advising / Counseling
Relevant "One-Liners":
No:

2   Advised people on How to conduct effective
    housing search + handle issues, as local
    resource person for group living

10 Consulted with scores of individuals on
    business writing, teaching them to analyze
    + present their experience

Skill Area " ": Researching Resources /
Relevant "One-Liners": Organizing Materials
No:

MARGO KELLER
3915 Derby Street
Berkeley, CA 94705
390-6554

OBJECTIVE: Public Information Specialist

SKILLS & EXPERIENCE

EDITING & WRITING
* Initiated and produced 12-24 page monthly newsletter for 24 consecutive issues.
* Wrote and self-published 23-page instructional manual, "Better Business Letters,"
  approved and used by professionals.
* Edited 100-page book on women's self-led career groups; co-authored group self-assess-
  ment questionnaire in widespread local use; developed series of informative hand-outs.

NETWORKING & RESOURCES
* Contacted hundreds of community agencies to update and index Counselors Resource Manual.
* Assembled library of materials and reports on cooperative living/working projects
  nationwide; used this to advise callers on how to make connections and find data.
* Developed greatly improved filing system for extensive engineering design materials.

ADVISING & TEACHING
* Advised hundreds of callers on how to conduct effective housing search and handle
  issues, as primary local resource person in collective-living field.
* Taught classes in: Typing & Office practice; Massage for Beginners; designed and taught
  6-session offering, "Field Visits to Bay Area Collective Homes."
* Consulted with scores of individuals on resume writing, teaching them to analyze and
  present their past experience in terms of current goals.

EMPLOYMENT HISTORY

1978-now   Keller Business Service: self-employed - resume, typing & editing services;
1975-1978 Editor - New Families-New Careers 1-Year Project - sponsor supported networking
1974   Administrative Asst/Technical Writer - LaRock-Market Engineers, San Francisco
1970-1973 Travel and independent study
1969-1970 Community Worker - Local employment offices, N.Y. State Labor Dept, Albany NY
1968-1969 Office Supervisor - Ager Finance Co, Gloversville, NY
           Director's Asst. & Instructor - OEO On-Job-Training Project,
           FMCC Community College, Johnstown NY

EDUCATION
State University of New York at Albany - 1967/68, Sociology

6

Tom Poole, Oakland

About the Author

DAMN GOOD RESUME SERVICE

The author works in Berkeley, doing one-to-one resume counseling and writing on a Macintosh computer. Readers living in the San Francisco Bay Area can call for an appointment and/or an informational brochure. Yana's work number is listed in the Oakland/Berkeley phonebook.

RESUME WORKSHOPS

Yana also presents one and two-hour workshops on resume writing at career development centers, job fairs, educational conferences and schools. If you would like her to speak to your group, feel free to call and discuss it.

NEW BOOK FOR COUNSELORS AND SERIOUS JOB HUNTERS

Check your local bookstore for THE RESUME CATALOG: 200 DAMN GOOD EXAMPLES, Yana's newest book (Fall 1987). It features hundreds of examples illustrating typical resume problems and offering some creative solutions for students, professionals, home-makers, immigrants and job hunters of all ages.

The Resume Catalog:

200 Damn Good Examples

by Yana Parker
Author of The Damn Good Resume Guide

Now we have the resource that people have been asking for—200 of the very best resumes from Yana Parker's files that put the principles of her book to work. It has *more resumes* than any other book. It has more *range and variety* than the other resume books. It is more *completely indexed* and *cross referenced* than any of the others. This adds up to an easily-used, dependable reference for anyone who wants to prepare a clear, positive presentation based on the ideas in DAMN GOOD RESUME GUIDE.

8½ × 11 inches   320 pages $9.95 paper

When ordering directly from the publisher, please include $1.00 additional for each book's shipping and handling.

TEN SPEED PRESS
P.O. Box 7123
Berkeley, California 94707

May we introduce other Ten Speed Press books you may find useful . . .
over three million people have already.

WHAT COLOR IS YOUR PARACHUTE?

By Richard N. Bolles. Based on the latest research, this new, completely revised and updated edition is designed to give the most practical step-by-step help imaginable to the career-changer or job-hunter whether he or she is sixteen or sixty-five. Questions asked throughout the cross-country research upon which this book is based, were: What methods of job-hunting and career-changing work best? What new methods have been developed by the best minds in the field? Is it possible to change jobs without going back for lengthy retraining?
6×9 inches, 416 pages, $8.95 paper, $15.95 cloth

WHERE DO I GO FROM HERE WITH MY LIFE?

By John C. Crystal and Richard N. Bolles. *New handy, smaller format/New cover* for this perennial favorite—*the workbook* for the self-motivated individual student or professional who has an interest in a systematic approach to career planning bringing together two of the leaders in the field.
7×9 inches, 272 pages, $9.95 paper.

WHO'S HIRING WHO

By Richard Lathrop. Because most people do not know the right steps to take in their job search most job seekers simply prolong their unemployment in their confusion. This book shows the new job seeker how to cope with today's market by utilizing job-hunting techniques which produce results.
6 x 9 inches, 272 pages, $7.95 paper.

THE JOB SHARING HANDBOOK

By Barney Olmstead and Suzanne Smith. Job sharing, the concept of two people equally sharing all elements of one job, is one of the ways in which people and organizations will cope with changing work conditions—fewer jobs, childbearing, special skills, senior citizens—all situations that require innovative responses. This book tells you how to take advantage of this new concept.
5½×8½ inches, 208 pages, $7.95 paper

You will find them in your bookstore or library, or can order them directly from us. Please include $1.00 additional for each book's shipping and handling.

TEN SPEED PRESS
P.O. Box 7123 • Berkeley, California 94707